**Someday
There Will Be
Machine Shops
Full of Roses**

**Someday
There Will Be
Machine Shops
Full of Roses**

Fred Voss

Smoke STACK BOOKS

Smokestack Books
1 Lake Terrace,
Grewelthorpe,
Ripon
HG4 3BU

info@smokestack-books.co.uk

www.smokestack-books.co.uk

Poems copyright
Fred Voss, 2023

ISBN 9781739772284

Smokestack Books
is represented
by Inpress Ltd

*These poems are for Joan,
the star I follow deep in my soul
my teatime raconteur
my diamond of wisdom and laughter
my longshot luck and blessing and dream
my lifelong friend and wife*

Acknowledgements

Some of these poems were previously published in the following magazines, anthologies and pamphlets:

The Earth and the Stars in the Palm of Our Hand (Culture Matters), *Robots Have No Bones* (Culture Matters), *Hard Labor* (with Don Winter, Working Stiff Press), *Teatime at the Bouquet Morale* (with Joan Jobe Smith, Liquid Paper Press), *Tooth and Fang and Machine Handle* (Liquid Paper Press), *Art That Roars* (Zerx Press), *Dwang* (Tangerine Press), *Singing for Another Revolution* (Tangerine Press), *Seeds of Fire* (Smokestack Books), *HWAET!* (Ledbury Poetry Festival), *Poetry Review* (London), *Fool-saint/Witch-pricker/Schizzo* (Tangerine Press), *Poetry London, The Morning Star, Litro, Mistress Quickly's Bed, Under The Radar, The Warwick Review, The Shop, Shakespeare N'a Jamais Fait Ca* (13E Note Editions, Paris, France), *Ambit, Pearl, Atlanta Review, Blue Collar Review, 5am, Nerve Cowboy, Swallow Dance, Bastille, The Art of Survival* (Kings Estate Press), *Beside the City of Angels* (World Parade Books).

Contents

Getting a Grip	11
Can Revolutions Start in Washrooms?	13
5-Minute Tough Guys	15
Interview #29	17
The Fist or the Butterfly	19
Wedding Rings and Tombstones	21
The Earth and the Stars in the Palm of our Hand	23
One of the Joys of Having a Wife Who's Still Alive	25
Saint Frank	27
Paycheque Babes	29
Today the Young People are Marching in the Streets	31
Better than Sigmund Freud's Couch	33
Cadillac Beasts	35
Blast Furnace at Midnight	37
No One Works as Hard as the Homeless	39
Another Kind of Beauty	41
Ready for a Vacation with Einstein	43
Missing Mussolini Parades and Mushroom Clouds	45
Looking for God as Jean Harlow Crosses Her Legs and Files a Fingernail While the Moon Watches	47
The Stranger in the Mirror	49
Half Machine	51
Einstein Rides a Beam of Sunlight into our Machine Shop	53
Hell in a Hardhat	55
The Luck in Steel Dust	57
No Room for Prometheus	59
My Father Reaches out for Me	61
Soul Washroom	63
Marilyn Before She Became Marilyn	65
Macbeth Wipes Turpentine Off His Fingers	67
Poetry Jackpot	69
Youngster Mankind	71
I'd Like to Thank the Machines	73
PhD School or Gang	75
Frank Almost Writes His First Poem About Paris	77

A Genius for Eating	79
The Pequod Sails Upon the Sea of Matrimony	81
Fist-Knock Future	83
No Room for Beethoven Kettle Drums	85
Timeless Wrench Brothers	87
Timeclock Supermen	89
Not Everyone Can Have a Nervous Breakdown in the Middle of the Mojave Desert	91
What is a Hammer Compared to the Heart of a Brother?	93
I Needed a Poem to Leap into My Brain and Bring Me a Woman	95
Trumpet Solo for Tomorrow	97
Wasn't Columbus a Bachelor?	99
Spark Spent: Mild-mannered Machinist	101
Who Needs Relativity When You've Got Dumpsters?	103
Charles Bukowski's Groupie	105
Art That Roars	107
A Thousand Secrets of Steel in His Fingers	109
Steel-Toed Soul	111
A Planet I Never Learned About in Any Book	113
Psychopaths Give Good Interviews	115
One Man Zoo	117
Solidarity in Hard Times	119
Beautiful as a Picket Line Under a Rising Sun	121
The Universe Can't Stop Laughing	123
Jim Morrison Thumbs a Ride On 4th Street	125
Ready to Go to Work	127
Turning Dillinger into Shakespeare	129
Laughter Lifeboat	131
Star-Spangled Purple Bandana General	133
Grow Back Green	135
Janis Joplin Never Belted Southern Comfort Bourbon and Screamed the Blues	137
Sure and Solid As Einstein	139
He Will Make Steel Sing	141
Champions	143
Robots Have No Bones	145
As Close as it Gets	147
Cary Grant	149

Always Ready to Grate Carrots	151
The Line No-One Crosses	152
What Good Is Gravity Without a Woman?	153
Gas Pumps and Metal Legs	155
Concrete Forest Floor	157
Someday There Will Be Machine Shops Full of Roses	159

Getting a Grip

Richard and Wes walk out
into the middle of the concrete floor between their machines
and square off
like they are in the middle of a wrestling ring
and SLAP
throw their palms together and lock thumbs
as the spindles of our machines hum with their cutters slicing
aluminium and steel
and we machinists all turn to watch
maybe
Richard can't get a grip on making his house payments
in his battle to keep his house from being foreclosed
because he hasn't had a raise in 4 years
maybe
Wes can't get a grip on his marriage because his low wage
keeps him from putting down the bottle
but Richard and Wes can have a grip contest
crouching and wrenching their arms about as their knees
begin to buckle
and they grind their teeth and grunt
trying to bring each other down
onto a rock-hard concrete floor
a man who lived in a cave once gripped the first spear
and hurled it into the side of an antelope
the opposable thumb
the key to club and handle and hammer and chisel and knot
and nail and wheel and pyramid and cathedral
closing around diamond or throat creating city
or balling into fist and starting
a war lifting baby
toward moon or digging
the first grave and Wes
is forcing Richard's knees closer to the concrete floor
as the tendons in Wes's and Richard's necks and wrists
stand out like cords

and they grunt and throw each other's arms back and forth
trying to make each other fall
maybe
they can't get a grip on politics
or nuclear war or Einstein's theory of relativity or why
we can't stop the seas from rising
maybe they can't get a grip on their lives
and keep them from falling apart
but they can lock fists and take it out on each other
and see who wins
even though somewhere deep in all our machinist hearts
we know
as the banks and the bosses and fat capitalist cats
and presidents beat us down
if we workers don't learn to come together soon
we're all
going to lose.

Can Revolutions Start in Washrooms?

I'm standing
in front of the washroom mirror washing up
after another day's work
all my life
I've seen the working man beaten down
unions broken
wages falling
as CEO salaries skyrocket and stockbrokers get rich
and politicians talk of 'trickle down'
and 'the land of opportunity'
and 'the American way'
and Earl on the turret lathe
keeps tying and retying his shoelaces that keep breaking
and blinks through 30-year-old glasses and finally
gives up his car
to ride the bus to work
and Ariel on the Cincinnati milling machines turns 72
heaving 80-pound vices onto steel tables
with swollen arthritic fingers and joking
about working until he drops
all my life I've wondered
why we men who've twisted chuck handles
until our wrists screamed
shoved thousands of tons of steel into white-hot blast furnaces
under midnight moons
leaned our bodies against screaming drill motors meeting
cruel deadlines until we thought
our hearts would burst
are silent
as the owners build their McMansions on hills and smoke big
cigars driving a different
$100,000 leased car to work each month
why after bailing out the banks
losing our houses
seeing our wages slashed

and our workloads rise
I've never heard one word
of revolt
and Teddy the bear of a gantry mill operator
walks into the washroom to wash
all the razor-sharp steel chips
and stinking black machine grease off
his arms and hands
he's been driving the same cheap motorcycle
for 20 years and says,
'Hey which front office person is driving
that brand new Jaguar I see parked out there now?'
and none of us can answer
as we raise our heads from the sinks
'Well, whoever it is,' Teddy says,
'They're making too much money!'

After 40 years of silence
I can't help wishing his words could be like the musket shot
that set off the storming
of The Bastille.

5-Minute Tough Guys

The men
from the offices are out on the shop floor
10 minutes before quitting time
watching us
to see if we are putting our tools away
4 or 5 minutes before the clean-up bell rings
and talking instead of working
and they fold their arms across their chests
and puff out their chests and stick their jaws out
to try to look tough and threaten us
but their feet are not sure
on the concrete floor
we
have stood on this floor for decades
planted our feet rock-solid and sure
as we lifted 100-pound vices
shoved 1-ton bars of heat-treated filthy steel
gritted our teeth and stood firm
and felt white-hot blast furnace flame lick our lips
the concrete floor is in our bones our groans
our shouts of 'Fuck!' to the tin ceiling 70 feet above
our midnight dreams our never-say-die smiles
we have passed out cigars at the birth of our baby boys on it
stuffed dollar bills into collection boxes for men who have lost
fingers to machine blades on it
laughed until our whole body shook
because if we didn't we might go insane on it
collapsed short of breath from 50 years of hammering and
hoisting and aching and sweating on it
and gone on
and on

how could those men from the plush-carpeted offices
with their soft hands and their soft souls
stand on it
with feet planted rock-solid and sure like ours
and as they stare at us
trying to look tough their feet fidget on the hard concrete floor
and give them away as they shift their legs
and blink their eyes and finally give up
trying to scare us
standing firm and tough and true
on a rock-hard gouged and pitted
stained-with-oil-and-sweat-and-human-blood concrete floor
isn't something you can learn to do in 5 minutes
it takes
a lifetime.

Interview #29

The supervisor has my job application in his hands
I sit in a little chair facing the supervisor's desk
and the supervisor pours
over my application like a dentist
looking for cavities
a detective
looking for crimes
I haven't worked in a year
I hear
the machines pounding and sawing and buzzing
outside the office's big glass windows
but I've almost forgotten
what it's like to stand in front of a machine
and grip its handles and pull down
a paycheque
my guts squirm my legs ache I'm in a cold sweat
trying to have the answers
to the questions before the supervisor asks them
and he looks up
and studies me
like a bug
in a jar
an amoeba
on a microscope slide
and I want to yell at him,
'Look, I'm a human being
I had a mother and a father who loved me
don't I have a right to eat
to have a bed and a roof over my head and a mailbox
and a toilet and an oven and a chair
to sit in with dignity and watch the sun go down safe
from rain and madmen's knives in alleys and jail cells
all I want to do is work
all I want to do is give you 10 hours a day and do whatever you ask
so I don't have to end up starving in the street'

but the supervisor is calm
he picks a piece of steak out from between his teeth
and flicks it at the floor
and studies me
waiting for me to crack under a bright white light
in fireplace factories
magnet factories gumball machine fire hydrant stovepipe
manhole cover gasket skateboard chair trashcan flashlight
parking meter bowling ball factories
across this land it is the same
supervisors
with big bellies and cold beady eyes
leaning back in soft leather chairs behind desks
holding our applications
and our lives
in their hands.

The Fist or the Butterfly

I push 2 aluminium slabs propped
against a red iron upright dolly
through the factory
2 slabs
¾" thick × 18' wide × 4' long weighing 100 pounds
leaned against my chest as my fist grips the red iron upright
dolly handle
and I push
with one hand the 100 pounds
and the dolly's 2 wheels roll across a grey concrete floor
and I swivel the dolly and the 2 slabs leaned against my chest
past workbenches and wooden crates
and steel I-beams to show
all the machinists how strong I am
when you work
every day with men who might suddenly fire a fist out of
nowhere
into your face it pays
to make a show of strength
but I wish at age 62 I could tell these men
the real strength
is in the curve of the petal
of a Van Gogh sunflower
the stunted broken legs of a dwarfed Lautrec rising
from a Paris suicide floor to turn off the gas
and paint the kicking legs of cancan dancers
the real strength
is in the shoes of Rosa Parks firmly planted on the floor
as she sits
in the front of the bus

Galileo
looking through his telescope telling us the universe
does not revolve around us
I want to tell these machinists in this factory the real strength
is not fists
or 18" necks or weightlifter chests
or the bomber planes we make
the real strength
is the swoop of the butterfly wing
around the rose
the real strength died on the cross
said, 'I have a dream'
I push
this 100 pounds of aluminium slabs resting against my chest
across a football-field-long building
to prove
what a man I still am
but at age 62
I am so tired of flexing muscles and closing fists and
pretending
the real strength
can't lie in the beautiful truth
of a poem.

Wedding Rings and Tombstones

We carved the stones
for cathedrals when men believed God was as real
as a redwood tree
we hammered the red-hot rivets
into bridges spanning wild rivers after Nietzsche said
God was dead
we made frames
for stretchers carrying men off bloody battlefields
bomb bay doors
dropping bombs that burn women alive
in hospital beds
we cut
steel holders for candles burning above the head of a mother
praying the operation
will save her daughter's sight feet
of 8th-story hotel bathtubs where opera divas
bathe hinges
for cell doors that close on men who must wait
for the electric chair combs
to shape the curl across the forehead of the movie star
who will soon cry as she holds the best actress Oscar
world wars come and go
Atlantic City casinos
rise and fall newsreels show the blinking eyes
of starved-to-skin-and-bone Auschwitz survivors
Neil Armstrong
sinks a boot into moon dust as we make
bedsprings and scalpels
trumpet mouthpieces and bulldozer teeth
a frying pan for Greta Garbo's
scrambled eggs and a cattle prod
for a torturer Alexander the Great
cries because he has no more worlds to conquer
Hitler shoots himself in his bunker
and people still need screwdrivers

and hairbrushes and we pick up our hammers
our wrenches our chisels as the sun rises
at 6.31am and the sweat
on our backs is still sweat and people
still need bowls and wheels
and kettledrums
the next baby to be born may be the man
to stop global warming or push
the button beginning World War 3
but the world will still need us to make wedding rings
and tombstones.

The Earth and the Stars in the Palm of our Hand

'Another day in paradise,'
a machinist says to me as he drops his time card
into the time clock
and the sun rises
over the San Gabriel mountains
and we laugh
it's a pretty good job we have
considering how tough it is out there
in so many other factories
in this era of the busted union and the beaten-down worker
but paradise?
and we walk away toward our machines ready
for another 10 hours inside tin walls
as outside perfect blue waves roll
onto black sand Hawaiian beaches
and billionaires raise martini glasses
sailing their yachts to Cancun
but I can't help thinking
why not paradise
why not a job
where I feel like I did when I was 4
out in my father's garage
joyously shaving a block of wood in his vice with his plane
as a pile of sweet-smelling wood shavings rose at my feet
and my father smiled down at me and we held
the earth and the stars in the palm of our hand
why not a job
joyous as one of these poems I write
a job where each turn of a wrench
each ring of a hammer makes my soul sing out glad for each drop of sweat
rolling down my back because the world has woken up
and stopped worshiping money
and power and fame

and because presidents and kings and professors and popes
and Buddhas and mystics
and watch repairmen and astrophysicists and waitresses
and undertakers know
there is nothing more important than the strong grip
and will of men
carving steel
like I do
nothing more important than Jorge muscling a drill
through steel plate so he can send money
to his mother and sister living under a sacred mountain
in Honduras
nothing more noble
than bread on the table and a steel cutter's grandson
reaching for the moon and men
dropping time cards into time clocks
and stepping up to their machines
like the sun
couldn't rise
without them.

One of the Joys of Having a Wife Who's Still Alive

Frank has begun to wonder
if he will regret not having loved Jane enough
after she's dead
if he will wish
he would have worn his red and green plaid
Christmas pyjama bottoms
that matched Jane's red and green plaid
Christmas pyjama bottoms
like she'd wanted him to
when they went to see their one-year-old great grandson
William
just flown over from England for Christmas
instead of feeling like it was too silly and sentimental a thing
for a poet who'd published 3 volumes of his poetry
to do
maybe he'll take out those red and green plaid
Christmas pyjama bottoms
as the dirt settles over Jane's coffin
and hold them grief-stricken
and wish he would have learned to dance
to Frank Sinatra records with Jane
like she'd always wanted him to
on those balconies of those inns on all their vacations
in San Francisco
instead of feeling like dancing to Frank Sinatra was something
a tough-as-nails 30-year-veteran machinist
just shouldn't do
and it will be too late
and he will put on one of their old Frank Sinatra records
and bury his face
in his red and green plaid Christmas pyjama bottoms
and weep
as the crows walk across Jane's grave
at 7am

Maybe,
but as Frank looks over at Jane next to him in bed this
Saturday morning
he leans over and kisses the beautiful hair on her sleeping head
and smiles

One of the joys of having a wife who's still alive
is not having to wear matching red and green
Christmas pyjama bottoms
or dance to Frank Sinatra.

Saint Frank

'What do you mean you wouldn't want to be poet laureate of
The United States?'
Jane asks Frank as they sip tea in bed Sunday morning
'I wouldn't want to have to suck up to an establishment
that condones continuous austere cutbacks
to The National Endowment for the Arts,'
Frank says proudly
lifting his nose in the air and sticking out his jaw like the man
who won't give information even under threat of being
tortured to death
'But you'd be getting an endowment to YOUR art
Poet laureates get stipends
They get grants and reading fees and you'd get flown all over
for free
and be feted and honoured and represent your country
and you'd sell hundreds and hundreds of your books!'
Frank shakes his head
and looks stubbornly at his pair of blue work jeans folded over
the chair and the hole
worn through one of its knees
like a badge of honour
'I wouldn't want to sell out'
Frank smiles proud of himself
like the last cop on a police force who can't be bribed
even though the rest of the cops threaten to cut his balls off
'I wouldn't want to represent a conservative academic
establishment that disrespects accessible narrative poetry'
'Whatta you mean Frank?
You just take the stipends
You just set your ideals aside for a bit and take the stipends
and then later bring your ideals back out again!' Jane says
looking over at Frank
so happy a million miles away rubbing shoulders with Galileo
and Socrates and Sir Thomas More and all the other heroes
and martyrs and saints

who've given up their freedom or their head or their life
for an ideal
'Okay Frank, drink your tea and have a good time with your
petty uptight recalcitrance,'
Jane says
as Frank smiles with self-satisfaction

After all,
no award is better for a man to turn down
out of a sense of honour
than one he stands almost no chance
of winning.

Paycheque Babes

We found ourselves
in families when we were babies
never really knowing how we got there
now
25 or 30 or 55 years later
we find ourselves in this machine shop
because we saw a help-wanted ad in a newspaper
or on a computer
we park
our toolbox at a machine we will spend more time next to
than our own wife
or child
and if we thought we had left our father far behind us in life
suddenly he comes barrelling
out of a glass bullpen in the figure of a foreman
telling us what to do
across the street from a graveyard
or a bowling pin factory or a tin building full of drop forges
pounding the earth with shock waves
and sending clouds of hot steam toward the sky
we try to make a home
next to each other
Buddhists atheists Vietnam veterans Vietnam war protesters
Guamanians Hungarians surfers
medical school dropouts gun lovers card casino addicts
murderers flying saucer believers
we bump into each other between our machines and try
to get along
brothers in machine grease and tapping fluid and cutter speed
and feed charts
and paycheques
we grow grey together
memorize the moles on the backs of each other's necks
watch each other tape photos of grandchildren
to our toolbox lids

mention our mother
starving in El Salvador or the Turkish sword
that murdered our grandfather in his backyard
in Armenia
as presidents and wars and hairstyles come and go
we laugh
whenever we can because there is gravity and television
and undertakers with bad toupees
bring in pans of eggrolls for everyone to eat
spar as our machines run like we are boxers
on the way to the top
ex-brahma bull riders ex-skid row winos ex-cons ex-Marines
survivors
of Haight-Ashbury or Scientology or knife-pulling wives
or crazy bosses
or loneliness
so sharp it almost slit our wrists we slap
each other's backs
as Friday paycheques are slipped into our hands
and stride out that tin factory door and fire up our cars
brothers of wrench and crane and muscle and sweat and grunt
heading for a horizon
that makes us all feel
like brand-new babes again.

Today the Young People are Marching in the Streets

The young are marching
young as the Golden Rule
the first human eye turned toward the heavens in wonder
young as a raindrop
a hammer blow cracking the Bastille
Blake
seeing his first angel
a knee is on our neck
but the young are shouting
strong and beautiful as Louis Armstrong's trumpet
Billie Holiday's croon
a knee is on the neck of the black man and the brown man
and the homeless man
and the homeless woman and the working man and the
working woman
a knee is on the neck of freedom
but the young are marching
young as Rosa Park's feet planted firmly
in the front of the bus
Frederick Douglas
wrestling his slave-master down to the ground
Joe Hill yelling, 'Organize!'
the dawn sun burning on Walt Whitman's open road horizon
a knee is on the neck of George Floyd and the poor
and the poem and Vincent Van Gogh with a sunflower
in his paintbrush
and this story is as old
as Bessie Smith's blues and James Baldwin's sad eyes
and every man
without hope who ever thought
of throwing in the towel but today
the young are marching in the street
marching for the homeless man trying to sleep on a sidewalk
the man from El Salvador

cheated out of his wages as he slaves
in a downtown L.A. sweatshop factory today the young
are marching and shouting and singing young
as Martin Luther King's dream
and the flame of the human spirit that must never
go out.

Better than Sigmund Freud's Couch

A machinist can form a relationship with a machine
he can lean
against it with his hand flat against the green side of its head
like he was leaning
against the side of a castle in a Mozart or Verdi opera and sing
an aria in manly basso profundo that echoes off the tin ceiling
70 feet above
he can dance
with it doing Fred Astaire whirls and tango steps as he throws
the machine's handles
as if they were the beautiful arms of Ginger Rogers
spray it
all day with Simple Green cleaner wiping it down
until it shines spotless
as he lines up his wrenches and hammers and callipers
on clean rags on his workbench
in front of it as if they were scalpels and forceps and saws
on an operating table and he was the heart surgeon
he'd once wanted to be looking
at the machine's digital readout numbers
as if they were blood pressure
and heart rate
or he can hunch
in a corner on a stool behind it setting up sheet metal
and cardboard walls around it
hiding
from eyes of supervisors and managers as if he'd pulled off
that 10 million dollar bank heist he saw
in a movie
a machinist may show his machine
tears on his face no human being has ever seen
speak to his machine insane dialogues
with himself no human being has ever heard
crawl on a concrete floor
blubber like a baby

let his eyes fill with insane fury
practice x-rated comedy routines he's never had the guts to do
on stage
at a comedy club
in front of a machine like he knows
the machine will forgive him
no matter what he thinks or does
perhaps even confess murders
no judge will ever know about
or write poems
that might be in anthologies 200 years from now

If machinists' machines could talk
even Sigmund Freud might go back to the drawing board
and start over.

Cadillac Beasts

The homeless are everywhere
sleeping and living on our sidewalks
in our alleys
under trees bridges and freeways in front of supermarkets
on beaches under mailboxes
on the steps of our churches
in our headlights
our madhouses
our jails
they grow more human
each day
holding out their bare palms on street corners
for our quarters and dollars
they are nothing
but blood
blinking eyes raw nerve
tired feet sore bone
flesh that grows cold and hot and burned and wet under sun
and rain and wind
hearts that ache
tongues that hunger souls
big as the sky with need
while in our sleek shiny cars
with our smartphones
our bank accounts our vacations to Cancun
we pass them calmly by like they aren't there
and as the sun goes down over our cities
the homeless shiver
and grow wiser and wiser
with suffering
while we grow madder and madder
with believing
they are there because they want to be
or deserve to be
these homeless

trying to remember when they were 3 years old
and a loving parent picked them up
and hugged them
like they would care for them
forever
these homeless
growing more and more human day after day
as we pass them by in our sleek shiny cars
each day becoming more and more
like beasts.

Blast Furnace at Midnight

I've had the morning taken away from me
assigned
to swing shift I have slept until noon so I could spend my time
working
until 1am
while others
dated women went to movies parties book launches
political rallies blues concerts A.A. meetings
I stood before a blast furnace
at midnight
feeling like I might never kiss another woman again in my life
supercilious supervisors
standing with clipboards in their hands calmly announced
that I was being moved to swing shift
and the sun was taken away from me
friends
no longer seen
sex
no longer a possibility I would punch out
long past midnight and drive home
through a dark city where everyone had gone out
and seen each other just hours before
and now slept
as the bars closed
and the cockroaches and mice came out
and only insomniacs and speed freaks
were awake
Kafka
is probably awake at this hour thinking about what a man
would feel like if he woke up a giant cockroach

Poe
clutching a pint of cheap whiskey in his fist
beginning to hear the tell-tale heart
of the old man he murdered pounding
through the floorboards
Bukowski
pouring beer and gritting his teeth because his woman
is out fucking
another man again
those supercilious supervisors
in their droning indifferent voice telling me
my life was being turned upside down
like they were merely telling me
to change my brand of toothpaste
never to see the sun rise
the mockingbird
and the raccoon my only friends
where was the Swing Shift Workers Society
holding keggers and dances until dawn
Thomas Edison is out in his garage
trying to invent the light bulb
Paul Revere about to get on his horse
Marx
dreaming of revolution
shipwrecked Robinson Crusoe
crawling up out of the surf to dig his fingers into the sand
of an unknown desert island
as I look out my window at Poe's raven croaking 'Nevermore'
and pick up this pen.

No One Works as Hard as the Homeless

For every ear-shattering WHAP of Frank's big hammer
smashing steel block down in vice
his wife Jane slides
a $5 bill into the palm of a homeless man or lady
in shadow of alley for every day
Frank spends wrestling
sharp-edged slabs of aluminium
and heaving 3-jawed 100-pound tool steel chucks
Jane slips
a $5 bill into the hand of a man from Mexico playing mariachi
on a purple squeeze box
on a downtown Long Beach Street corner or a woman
with nothing but a blanket and her outstretched palm
on a dirty sidewalk
no one works as hard as the homeless
hiking up and down alleys all day and night
searching our trash dumpsters
pulling out bottles and tin cans
pushing them into giant plastic bags they fill and hoist
over their shoulders and haul over bridges
toward recycling centre dimes
so they can get a loaf of bread
as CEOs
sit in offices bigger than luxury apartments daydreaming
about their golf games or their next vacation in Biarritz
no one works as hard as the homeless
somehow remembering how to smile
walking hundreds of miles a week combing our alleys
for scraps of food
somehow going on
living on raw will and air and a chess game
or a bottle of cheap vodka shared
in a park or under a freeway overpass
and Jane pays them
for every chip of red-hot steel

flying off razor-sharp cutter to land on Frank's neck
smoking
Jane is sliding a $5 bill into the palm of a man or woman
on the edge of giving up hope
and dying
because no one works as hard as the homeless
taking the next step
when no one cares
no one works as hard as the homeless
never stopping
barely sleeping
hardly knowing where to turn next
as they hold onto each $5 bill Jane gives them
like it was all that was left
of human kindness.

Another Kind of Beauty

The young woman
stands at the Bridgeport mill
in the cold machine shop morning air
she has pulled the hood of her jacket over her head
baggy work pants and shirt big work boots cover her body
only her face and hands stick out for us men machinists to see
and they are beautiful
but the razor-sharp cutter fits her hands
the cutter holder
in the machine spindle fits her palm as her fingers wrap
around an Allen wrench
and tighten the holder's locknut
onto the cutter with all the muscle
in her arm and back
and she is not here for us to see her shapely body
or shiny long black beautiful hair
she is Rosa Parks firmly planting her black feet
in the front of the bus
Norma Rae
defying the bosses standing up on her textile factory
workbench holding the 'UNION' sign
high above her head
for all the workers to see
Spartacus
leading the slave rebellion Emma Goldman
leading the suffragettes King
leading the freedom march out of Selma
because we are all
human beings
unbeaten unbroken
her smile
unstoppable as the sunlight breaking through
a storm cloud
her hands
turning machine handles like

she was born to turn them
the young woman is inevitable
as the Grand Canyon revolutionary
as Galileo's telescope beautiful
as Madam Currie accepting
the Nobel Prize and every dream that ever
came true.

Ready for a Vacation with Einstein

The timeclock
ticking in the corner of the factory where we work
must have been invented in a monastery
where life was so boring some monk decided
time should be divided up
into always-exactly-the-same-length absolutely equal seconds
and since then without one shred of feeling
that timeclock has ticked
through the years and centuries
ticked
as old men collected stamps
and Jack the Ripper butchered another woman in a London alley
and Pavlova danced Swan Lake in Paris
and the Enola Gay dropped its atom bomb
aimed at Hiroshima
ticked
as cash registers rang and men on death row
looked at calendars and we
punched into this timeclock made aircraft spars
or motorcycle sidecar yolks
or electric guitar volume knobs
ticked
through world wars and Beethoven symphonies and heart operations and haircuts
as if our lives and this universe were nothing
but a huge pile
of timeclock ticks
but didn't time stop
to catch its breath each time Marilyn Monroe
took a step across the screen
didn't time stop
to weep as Sophocles' plays in the library at Alexandria
burned

didn't time turn around and want to go backwards
after Martin Luther King
was shot
doesn't time go running down the middle of a street
at midnight screaming
each time a man or woman loses
their mind
and what timeclock could have borne ticking
through Christ's last breaths
and the cat knows we are fools
as he sits atop a stack of old tires in the sun
behind this factory
his eyes timeless
as Da Vinci's Mona Lisa
and our hearts
the minute the end-of-the-workweek quit-work whistle blows
and we race out the building away from that timeclock
toward a vacation on a black sand beach in Hawaii
where we sip Pina Coladas
with Einstein as he shakes his wild hair
in four-dimensional space
and says timeclock time is nothing
but an illusion.

Missing Mussolini Parades and Mushroom Clouds

Perhaps it is best
we spend our lives between these blank tin walls
outside
Hitler combs his moustache the Great Barrier Reef
dies Jack the Ripper
sharpens his butcher knife
all we have to do is learn how to not go mad after 30 years
between these blank tin
machine shop walls listening to 100,000 timeclock ticks
outside
a hospital full of children is bombed
as Nero tunes his fiddle
perhaps it is best
no one cares what we think
or wants to interview us or put our picture
on the the front page of a newspaper
as Trump swoops his hair across his bald head
and grins at himself in the mirror
while the Atlantic Ocean prepares to swallow New York City
perhaps it's good
our days are made of drops of oil out of our oilcans
swings of our wrench
blows from our hammer
basic as the foundations of all the houses and the white lines
running down the middle
of all the highways
perhaps it is good we stand at our machine all day trapped
between these tin walls
missing
Mussolini parades and mushroom clouds
and rockets to Mars as the last lion roars
the only blood on our hands
our own
when a finger gets too close to a cutting edge or a saw blade

we will never become famous
escaping from a straightjacket underwater
like Houdini
or sell coffee makers on tv like Joe DiMaggio
or have a million people throw confetti
out of windows onto our head in a tickertape parade
our lives
are tape measures and sweaty arms
and piles of oily bronze chips
eyes outside these tin walls will never see
never want to see
but we make it through one minute one hour one day one
decade after another behind
these tin walls
and somehow manage to smile
smiles bright as the morning sun
as Hitler hidden in his bunker
puts the gun to his head and pulls
the trigger.

Looking for God as Jean Harlow Crosses Her Legs and Files a Fingernail While the Moon Watches

We have looked for God
in the sky
formulas words mathematical proofs eclipses and on
mountaintops in miracles and rocket ships
to the moon we have sat in caves churches classrooms
dissected cats put together clocks
torn apart roses built pyramids wrapped mummies
sacrificed lambs wound watches worn black
dragged giant stones across Easter Island
pointed radio telescopes
toward galaxies full of stars worshipped Elvis
looking for God
waiting for God
whispering prayers to God
we forgot
the pebble in the gutter in St. Louis
the hat at the Dry Cleaner in Chinatown the horn
of the rhinoceros the button
on Lincoln's shirt the thread of the spider
the drip of the stalactite the drop
of water gleaming on Marilyn Monroe's right breast
the silence
inside a box factory the sound inside a seashell
the shoelace of Joe Louis the shadow
of the snail confetti
on the ballroom dance floor
after the last New Year's Eve party horn
blows
we have looked for God
in stained glass windows entrails of birds mitres of bishops
holy grails
and squashed grapes but we forgot
the dust

inside a bell that hasn't rung for a thousand years
the ant
crawling across a death row cell at dawn
the smell of the train wheel
skidding to a stop on the track so Martin Luther King can say,
'I have a dream!' the card
Edgar Allen Poe played when he lost his last dime
the ring on the finger of the strip club drummer
smashing his drumstick into a cymbal
as Gypsy Rose Lee peeled off
a glove the comb
Albert Einstein never picked up for the last 20 years
of his life
the Museum of Natural History
night watchman sipping tea and looking up
at the bones of the 65-million-year-old Tyrannosaurus Rex
skeleton
at 3am like those bones are his last friends
we forgot the marbles rolling out of the fingers of 5-year-old
boys who know they can dig a hole
to China and junkyards
full of hubcaps and spark plugs
we forgot
the zebra's stripe the trumpet in the Chicago pawn shop
window Buster Keaton's
porkpie hat and Jean Harlow
crossing her legs and filing a fingernail as the moon
watches and the streetcar rings
its bell
for every man and woman who ever
lived.

The Stranger in the Mirror

A year goes by
5 years
12 years
we say good mornings
to each other give each other thumbs-up signs laugh
at our bad haircuts or toupees
talk about
football scores or dual carburettors or the length of shark teeth
or what we feed our pet pythons
until one day
I look up
and realize Carl has gone grey
Troy has a limp from all the years
walking across the machine shop concrete floor Armando
is curving at the shoulders after all the years
bending over his engine lathe Tadeusz
no longer laughs Harry
has grown angry
about everything
since his son gave up trying to make the major leagues in
baseball
and writing a thousand poems about machine shops
has put a spring in my step
because I've grown to love
my job
we are growing old together
as earthquakes and solar eclipses and stock booms and busts
and dance crazes and world
heavyweight boxing champions come and go
we are growing old together
as the timeclock ticks
and we tell each other the latest joke
or watch the latest goofy You-tube
video together
as our machines run

one of us could be slowly going insane
or flirting with suicide or finding poetic fame
in England or growing to believe God
talks to him each morning
through a shower nozzle
and we'd never know it
through all the Christmas parties and supervisor speeches
and turning gears and sharpened cutters
we look up
and suddenly one of us has a face cross-hatched with lines
or trembles in his fingertips
or hasn't smiled in years
we look up
and 2 or 3 decades have passed
as the cutting oil drips from our fingers and we look
into a washroom mirror and try to remember
to tell ourselves
hello.

Half Machine

Sometimes a machinist stops talking
to other machinists
he stares for months at a tin wall as the spindle on his machine
sends a 50-tooth saw cutter
chewing through steel or a drill bit spiralling
through brass
maybe
his wife died or is divorcing him or the winning horse
he's counting on never saves him or he is worried
about the sea's coral reefs dying or something his father said to
him 20 years ago
is sinking its teeth into his heart
trying to kill him
he runs his fingers through the drawers of his toolbox fondling
screws and crescent wrenches
and pieces of steel shim stock
and never talks
maybe he is sitting on a barstool in his mind
dreaming the love of his life
will finally walk through the barroom door
in a short skirt and a green hat
and save him
or that he will finally write a song on his guitar
that will reach #1 on the radio
but it's like he's become
half machine
like he's leaving
the human race
and becoming molybdenum steel like his wrench
trigonometric table decimals like the ones he uses to calculate
machine cutter paths
maybe no matter what he does
he can't quit using
cocaine
or maybe he thinks he should become

a woman
but perched on his steel stool his head is so high in the clouds
he can look down
on Everest
his fist squeezing a hammer handle
his eyes locked on his machine's rotating spindle
no 'hello' or 'what's up?'
reaches him
as his eyes burn with a twinkle further away
than the stars at the edge of the universe
he is tool steel
and cutting oil and what's deep deep inside him
something
none of us will ever
know about
something only a man
who is half machine
can understand.

Einstein Rides a Beam of Sunlight into our Machine Shop

I was amazed when one day a machinist came to work wearing
a T-shirt
with a big photo of Albert Einstein on it
with his wild hair and his twinkling
stoned-on-the-universe eyes
as if Einstein were a rock star to rival Jim Morrison
but then
I thought why couldn't a machinist
who worked with machine speed and feed equations
and memorized drill charts and carved perfect curved convex
10-inch radiuses across the face of shining steel blocks
be fascinated
by Einstein's idea
of space bent by gravity
why shouldn't a machinist
who watches a beam of dawn sun shoot
over a mountain top through a machine shop tin door
onto the red long-necked oilcan sitting
on top of his engine lathe each morning want
to ride a sunbeam
like Einstein when he found that nothing was faster than light
didn't Einstein like to sit in a boat in the middle of a lake
with a paper hat on his head
contemplating curved space
all day
the way a machinist in his hardhat sitting on a stool watching
a cutter turn
all day
contemplates the curve of a wave he will ride
Sunday
and didn't Einstein love sex
and stick his tongue out at a camera in a world-famous photo
didn't Einstein love to laugh at Charlie Chaplin's tramp
and like to wear a rumpled sweatshirt like

the one a machinist loves to wear
didn't Einstein love to listen to himself play the violin
the way a machinist loves to listen to the singing
of steel he is shaving
with the 7-degree tip of a razor-sharp cutting tool
I'm sure Einstein would have been happier
keeping his mouth shut turning the handles
of a machine than trying to think of small talk
at a university cocktail party
and working in a machine shop all day
he could have talked to us machinists
about Spinoza's idea
that God is everywhere even in a drop of black tapping fluid
or the swinging of a wrench hanging from a workbench nail
or the heart of a machinist
who can laugh watching Charlie Chaplin's little tramp
twirl his cane
or shed a tear
listening to a Beethoven
violin

maybe next week I'll walk into the machine shop
wearing a T-shirt covered with the portrait
of Shakespeare
men who are able to contemplate curved space
ought to be able to enjoy
a good swordfight.

Hell in a Hardhat

I still think of that 1950s hero The Lone Ranger
with his mask
'Who was that masked man?' everyone in the tv show asked at the end
as The Lone Ranger rode away
triumphant and anonymous again
and Superman
fooling Lois Lane year after year with his Clark Kent glasses
stepping into the phone booth
to put on his big 'S' Superman shirt
I'm a poet
but no one here in this machine shop knows it
never
in a million years will a Van Gogh hang on the machine shop tin wall
or a machinist open a book of Robert Frost
while he chomps on a burrito full of red-hot chili peppers
and stares at a photo of a woman in a string bikini
draped across the hood of a red Mustang
Dante
might walk down into Hell to see men without heads
but he would never put on a machinist apron to open the pointed jaws of a micrometer
inside a jackhammer casing
Pablo Neruda the great Chilean poet
who read his poetry in stadiums
full of tens of thousands of people
had to flee
the government on horseback over the Andes mountains
because he was so famous
and dangerous
in Russia
Osip Mandelstam died in a prison camp
because he likened Stalin's moustache
to a cockroach

here
in America I hide
smuggling
the lives of all these remarkable unknown working men
out the tin door in poems
I publish in England
lives
that may be read about 100 years from now
so men and women can remember
what these machines were like
and how we treated
the men who ran them
so badly
I may not have to escape on horseback
or die in a prison camp
but like Dante
I've descended into a kind of Hell
it's just that in my Hell
instead of swallowing a red-hot ball of iron
you might have to wear
a hardhat.

The Luck in Steel Dust

43 years ago
when I quit writing about TS Eliot in English literature
graduate school to work
in a gasket factory and a steel mill
next to ex-cons and bronco bull riders
men who dropped out of 8th grade and could barely read
and would have used a book of Shakespeare plays
as a coaster for a mug full of beer
I felt like a failure
never had a man admitted to a PhD program at UCLA
fallen so far
and I cut my vocabulary in half
and glowered and balled up my fists and swaggered around
on the concrete floor
like I had just stepped out of a prison cell
I'd shared with John Dillinger
and dragged myself through my days with ball peen hammer
and blast furnace flame
and hardhat and black steel dust stink up my nostrils
and under my fingernails
until one day I wrote a poem about it
and now
3,000 poems later they say I am unique and remarkable
because I chose
to go into the factories and turn it
into literature
now what once made me wish I were dead
may make me live forever
in a history book
where I rub shoulders with Melville and Hemingway
and Jack London
men of action who lived what they wrote
and I am proud every time I grip a wrench
or a micrometer
does the caterpillar know

it will become a butterfly
did Einstein know his equation $E=mc^2$
would explode an atom bomb
or Robert Stroud know picking up a starving baby bird
in a prison yard turn him
into The Birdman of Alcatraz
did the oxygen molecule know 2 molecules of hydrogen
would make it water
did Van Gogh know how he made a sunflower live
on canvas
does the bluebird understand why it's song
is beautiful
and I close my fingers around the handle of my hammer
and smile
sometimes a man just has to take the luck
that's handed to him
and try not to pretend he knew
what he was doing.

No Room for Prometheus

We are filling up the world with words
screws black hole theories selfie photos
tweets texts egos
tires telescopes rants celebrity smiles top
100 lists weather predictions where is a person as still
as a tree
a penniless Van Gogh painting an immortal sunflower
in solitude
the 10-billion-year sparkle
of a star Nirvana
older than sound
a boat
just floating Jupiter
just turning the butterfly wings silently folded
inside the chrysalis we are filling
the world with opinions
plastic bags haircuts Googles pundits
puddings profits exhaust pipes Armageddons robots
Prozacs beaver shots Dolby movie explosions Oscar races
Rotor Rooter emergencies
rising seas karate chops communion wafers golf carts
swizzle sticks and swastikas where
is the blank page
waiting for the next Blanche Dubois
the silence
inside Charlie Parker's saxophone the moment
before he found bebop
where is Whitman's wild beard
as he walks down his open road
with nothing in his pockets
we are filling the world
with toothpastes toys tirades smokestacks surfboards
gearshifts cereal brands talk shows psychological disorders
bullet trains bullseyes bell curves soap operas
and elephant tusk souvenirs

where is that long long dark empty night
filling Prometheus's soul the moment before
he discovered
fire?

My Father Reaches out for Me

Gustavo often stared at me
across the wide concrete shop floor
now he is dead
they will lower him into the ground tomorrow
I should have talked to him
I should have climbed into that convalescent home deathbed
and hugged my father
when he reached out his arm to me
instead of just shaking his hand
so many times
I passed Gustavo's beautiful photographs of waterfalls and
rocks and canyons and rivers
he taped to the side of his toolbox
and wondered about his sad Cherokee face
and only said 'Hello' to him
so many times he stared at me across the hundred feet
between our machines
like he could read my poet's heart
as well as he could take those beautiful photographs
but we never talked
when my father lay in his convalescent home deathbed
if only I had hugged him like I used to do when I was 2
and not been afraid at age 33 to cry
on his chest because we only ever have
one father
not stood there shaking his hand trying to act strong and adult
and now the company president gathers us workers in a circle
around Gustavo's toolbox
and asks us to bow our heads
in a moment of silence
and Gustavo is not dead
his sad eyes
look at me across the wide concrete floor
and I hug my father now
I hug my father and cry like a baby against his chest

because he was all the God
I would ever know
and I look over at Gustavo's toolbox
where 6 candles burn
and his last photographs
of river and waterfall
we have only just barely begun to live
this life.

Soul Washroom

In the employee washroom
we can barely hear the presses pound
the warm water out of the faucets is soothing
to our aging fingers and we let it run
over them until our bones are warmed as we stand at sinks
the supervisors
and the stink of rusty burnt steel and the screaming of the
saws and the shock waves
off 2-ton drop hammers are far away as we stand
elbow to elbow at mirrors and look for new grey hairs
in our beards or lines on our faces
'I haven't had a decent hard-on in years,' old Earl says
and we all laugh and someone else says,
'I try to stay out of trouble but it keeps looking for me,
or it's down at the end of the road waiting for me,'
and we all nod
as close as we can get to letting down our guards
as we begin to talk of our homes that are worth less
than we owe on them
daughters
who won't speak to us
fathers
we last saw when they punched us in the face
when we were 17
as we scrub our fingers in the white gravelly Boraxo soap
until our hands disappear in the white soothing soapy foam
and we begin to feel like we might actually wash away
all the dirt and pain
of all the years
train bulls that came at us with clubs
when we had to ride the rails
ex-wives
that took half our money and left us living in tiny trailers
beside railroad tracks
all the firings all the long shot horses

that never came in stocks that crashed
long lost Iraq War soldier sons
or holy Guatemalan mountains
we'll never see again until it feels
for one second like a man's arm might even go around another
man's shoulder until
we have to screech those faucets shut
and all that warm soap and water is gone down the drain
and we stick
our jaws and chests back out and march
out the washroom door onto a blackened cracked concrete
floor where never in 50 years
has there fallen
one tear.

Marilyn Before She Became Marilyn

Marilyn
is walking down the concrete aisle past our machines
before
she was Marilyn
those legs
that walk
don't take that screen test
I want to tell her
stay a secretary
carrying papers down a factory aisle
and I'll never set another poem down on paper
we'll marry
we'll wake up in the morning to have tea
the sunlight on your ankle
will be more beautiful than anything Michelangelo
ever dreamed of carving into marble
we will clink teacups
that smile
a million people will never see
all mine
the poems
I will never write all yours
as I kiss you
you'd be like you were in *The Misfits*
when for the first time you took off
your Marilyn Monroe mask
a little girl
needing love
and I will write all my poems with my fingers
on your flesh
and we will ride into work snuggled together in my 1957 Ford
someone should make a movie about us
the workers will say
as they see us walking so happy side by side across the gravel
parking lot

into the factory
and I will stand at my machine and carve steel down
into love poems
to you all day
as you walk down the concrete aisle carrying a work order
to the Blanchard Grinder operator
so all the men chained to their machines can know
there's a heaven
on earth.

Macbeth Wipes Turpentine Off His Fingers

I made this life
Shakespeare
and rolling overhead 10-ton cranes run by men in hardhats
who think
Shakespeare was a fag
hex nuts
and blue/green coolant splashing across tool steel cutting
edges sharp enough
to cut heat-treated steel like butter as Macbeth
goes sleepless
a 3rd night straight
and Mexicans
on milling machines talk about the way the boxers on tv
throw punches
no job ad
in the paper for a machinist poet read,
'Excellent opportunity
for a good man who can set up a machine to look for poems
among piles of smoking steel chips'
no class at a university was offered to show me
how to find literature inside a barrel full of dirty shop rags
smelling of turpentine
and grease
dropped
out of UCLA PhD school in English literature I stumbled
into a steel mill and sweat for 7 years
before the first poem
came to me
from hiss of cutting torch and flame of blast furnace
and feeling
like I couldn't go on
another day
I made this life
poem by poem and aircraft part by aircraft part
until opening my toolbox as the start-work whistle blows

is a thing of joy
as 72-year-old Tadeuz
sharpens the cutting edge of the cutting tool
on the diamond grinding wheel
his whole body
dancing from toe to fingertip as he turns that razor-sharp tool
against that wheel
and carves out the end
of this poem.

Poetry Jackpot

I wish the machinists around me in this shop
could feel the joy
I feel
each morning as I wait for the poems to come to me
like the black machine grease from the steel joints
of my machine oozing
across my fingers
motors
firing up all across the concrete floor
men
swaying their whole bodies as they hold
big aluminium aircraft tubes like tubas in their arms
and dance with them scraping them
in circular motions across huge discs
of super-coarse blue sandpaper glued
to workbench tops for hours and hours
until all that scraping sounds like the Grand Canyon
being carved out
Roy
from Texas not speaking to Gabriel from Colombia
on the next machine for over
3 years
I cannot wait to open my toolbox each morning
and look for poems
on such things while these machinists
around me drag their feet like they are dead because they feel
doomed
to work in this factory the rest of their lives while they dream
of winning the California State Lottery jackpot
and escaping
Who said there was no magic elixir
of life?
Each turning of a machine wheel
magic
each minute

a gift
I look for poems
in the chip
of steel spiralling up off the cutting edge
on a smoking ¼-20 tap
or 74-year-old Jorge
throwing open the steel machine shop door BANG
to let in the cold 6.04am air and look
at the new coat of snow on the San Gabriel mountains
he loves to look at as he tugs on a rubber belt
shifting gears in his machine's head
Who cares if a poem makes no money
when it keeps you
alive?

Youngster Mankind

It never gets old
the moment Friday when the end of the week quit-work
whistle blows
the sky
suddenly so blue
the soap
washing the black machine grease off our fingers
suddenly so sweet we drop
time cards into the slots of time clocks in that moment
that never
gets old
each note
of our favourite song ringing truer than ever
the sea
so alive with fish
it is the moment that makes all the hours and hours and hours
on grinding machines and drop hammers
worth it
the moment
when Seabiscuit came racing from the back of the pack
to thread through all the horses
and win
when Franklin Roosevelt
rose on his polio-stricken legs in braces to somehow walk
across a political convention stage to a microphone
and run
the moment
the Berlin wall broken into rubble by the sledgehammers
of a cheering crowd
fell
the moment
the shell-shocked
WWI amnesia victim left for lost in some hospital room
for years suddenly remembered
his name

and we grip our lunch pails
and head toward the sun shining through a factory doorway
to stride across this earth where that youngster mankind
has barely begun
to live.

I'd Like to Thank the Machines

Ever since I entered the factories it has been me
vs. the machines
mastering their dials
their universal heads rpms gearshifts stops
quills vices chucks coolant tanks
crankhandles
and then the computer chip revolution
and it all
means nothing
as I must learn it all over again
with computer control panel buttons
to punch
after 30 years as a machinist will the next computer chip
revolution try to take away
my job
again?
but the machines have been good to me too
I've never had to shake their hand or smile at them
or act like I like them
when I want to kill them
they've let me be
when I've had horrible hangovers
when women have dumped me leaving me feeling like I want
to die
they've stood by me
noble with their green steel heads and sides and their coolant
hoses
endlessly pouring coolant for me
they've let me sit beside them on a steel stool for hours writing
these poems
in my head
they've screamed in my ear
until I ground my teeth all night
ripped into steel razor-sharp parts and hurled them like
bullets

past my head until my heart
leaped
still they let me dream
of Marilyn Monroe's legs
or Galileo
dropping those 2 iron balls off the leaning tower of Pisa
they could cut off my fingers
or let me write 10,000 poems
it's all the same to them
still
if I ever win the Nobel Prize for literature
I'll make sure to thank
the machines.

PhD School or Gang

Ramon
is half my age and he never speaks a word to me
tattoos
on the back of his neck make me wonder
about gangs
I never spoke
my first years in the machine shops dropped out of the UCLA
PhD program in English literature and wishing
I was dead
everyone around me wondering
if I was going to suddenly pull out a knife
or a gun
so I step up to Ramon's machine where he has set a shell mill
shaving
through a 100-pound block of steel until that steel shines
like glass and say, 'Nice finish,'
and run my finger over the smoothness of the steel
and nod to let him know he has set that shell mill spinning
at the perfect rpm and he nods and smiles
and I know he will never pull out a gun
I lend him my special Starrett edge finder
and see the gentle way he handles it
like he could never drop it
and know he means well just like me
I help him pick up the 100-pound block of steel
so his back can never be hurt
and he smiles with a warmth in his eyes that tells me
no matter what violent barrio he may have grown up in we can still
work as one
every inch
of his body speaks to me as we set the block of steel down
on a workbench
and his chest swells with pride
at my old man master machinist approval

of his skill
PhD school
or gang
we all have our wounds in this life
to overcome
and who needs words anyway
when hugging 100-pounds of filthy greasy steel
can make men close
as brothers.

Frank Almost Writes His First Poem About Paris

'Please, Frank,
nearly every poem you write has a concrete floor in it,'
Jane says
after Frank reads her his new poem about a machine shop
with a concrete floor in it.
'You've got to write about something else, Frank, something
not so arduous.
Write about our trip last summer to Paris.
We saw the Eiffel Tower and original Van Goghs
and Cezannes and Notre Dame
and boated down the Seine
and saw a surrealistic statue of Rimbaud
James Joyce's original manuscript of *Ulysses*
at Shakespeare and Company
and visited Jim Morrison's grave.
Why don't you write about Paris? Something romantic.'
'But that's such a cliché!
Everyone who goes to Paris sees Notre Dame and the Louvre
and Eiffel Tower
and takes boat rides down the Seine
and sees Morrison's grave and writes about it.
If readers want romance they can read *Madame Bovary*.
Let them read *Les Miserables*.
No one's ever written about greasy shop rags
or piles of metal chips
on a concrete machine shop floor the way I have!
Did Flaubert or Hugo or Baudelaire write
about a machinist spitting a sunflower seed
over the top of an engine lathe
or riveting a 'World Class Asshole' plaque
to the inside of his toolbox lid?'
Frank takes a big chug from his bottle of beer
and sticks out his chest
like Ernest Hemingway.

'Writers should write what they know! What they live!
Not clichés of boating down the Seine,
ogling art and an Eiffel Tower!'
Frank smiles a self-satisfied smile
until he sees Jane
glaring up at him from her chair like she always does
when it's obvious he's full of crap
and Frank sips more beer and remembers
their sunset walk alongside the Seine
their fondant au chocolate and champagne
at the sidewalk café
in sight of the Eiffel Tower
the Paris July 8 full moon on his birthday
shining into the skylight
of their bedroom in their *autrement* on Rue Beautrellis.

After all, Frank does have to admit
that it is just possible, that for just one poem anyway
to write about lamp-lit, rain-streaked cobblestone streets
and the way the summer sun sparkling
between Notre Dame's steeples
turned Jane's auburn hair to a golden flame
could be just a bit more interesting,
possibly even more romantic than
a sunflower seed spit over the top of an engine lathe
onto a concrete floor
and a 'World Class Asshole' plaque.

A Genius for Eating

'It's so great that you love my cooking so much!' Jane says
to Frank as she serves him dinner in bed
'No one else ever loved my cooking before
I get to cook my food for you
and you love to eat it!'
Frank sits up in bed watching his favourite movie *Vertigo*
as Jane hands him the tray with the dinner
she's cooked for him on it
big golden brown
turkey leg in wonderful-smelling golden gravy
with homemade delicious stuffing
and steamed broccoli
and a big piece of Jane's homemade pumpkin pie beside it
and as he bites into the juicy delicious turkey leg
Frank thinks
how great it is
in order to make Jane deliriously happy
all he needs
is a tongue
and taste buds and salivary glands and throat and intestines
moving in peristaltic motion swallowing
and a stomach to receive and digest
his other skills took decades of hard work
to perfect
micrometers and C-clamps and overhead cranes
and machine handles
and a 1,600-page Machinery's Handbook
full of speeds and feeds and thread pitch diameters
and tap drill diameter calculations
and trigonometry and metallurgy and 100-pound vices
he had to lift and crazy foremen
he had to let scream in his face
and images and metaphors and syntax and rhythms
he had to devise
or wait to receive from the muse

as he gradually
carved out over the years his own territory and style
as the world's first machinist poet
surviving
firings and long-term unemployment and machinists
threatening to meet him
in the parking lot with knives and rejections
by poetry magazine editors that made him feel
like he should never have lifted
a pen
now all Frank has to do is say,
'This turkey is the best I've ever tasted in my life!'
and mean it
and Frank works out a little running his tongue
around the inside of his mouth
as he perfects licking gravy off his teeth and smiles

After shoving hundreds of tons of steel bars
into the roaring white-hot flames of blast furnaces
it's nice to have a skill that only requires sliding
a turkey leg
into his mouth.

The Pequod Sails Upon the Sea of Matrimony

As he has every night for 4 months
Frank is reading *Moby Dick*
(a novel he has read 5 times)
to Jane before they go to sleep.
Having reached chapter 72 he reads details
of how a whale is stabbed and speared
again and again at close range
by laughing pipe-smoking sailors until the whale
spouts blood
and rolls over and the sailors carve up its blubber
and cut off its head
and gather whale vomit.
Frank smiles and says, 'Melville's detailing of the tools
and skills of whaling is just like what I do
with the machine shop in my poems,'
as Jane sighs and bites her fingernails.
'Frank, please stop,' Jane says. 'I can't take anymore.
I can't even swim. We've got to get off the Pequod.
I want romance.
I want you to read to me from MY BOOK now.'
Frank winces
and reaches for Jane's pretty little book *Elizabeth and Philip*
in which he has reached chapter 2 and reads
of their royal wedding on November 20, 1947
wedding presents
rings and jewellers
wedding gown with rose-and-corn-ear-patterned lace pink
carnation floral decorations
chauffeurs and royal coaches and The King's Valet
and what the Huntley and Palmers wedding cake was made of
and how much it weighed
are detailed and analysed to Jane's smiling anglophile delight.
Frank and Jane look at the photographs
of Elizabeth and Philip
standing at the Westminster Abbey altar waving

out the windows of the Cinderella carriage
smiling from the Palace balcony.
'Oh wasn't Elizabeth beautiful!
Royal weddings are so romantic!' Jane gushes
as Frank writhes and slaps shut the pretty little book
unable to take any more and eager for tomorrow night
when he can get back to the fun and pleasure
reading *Moby Dick*
with tattooed-all-over shrunken-head-carrying
cannibal Queequeg
and a giant albino whale
who methodically saws off Captain Ahab's leg and drowns
sailors with a slap of its tail
and finally rams and sinks the Pequod itself
in the middle of the Pacific Ocean
leaving Ishmael afloat on Queequeg's coffin
like an orphan ready to be rescued
by the ship Rachel looking for its lost sailors.
Now what royal wedding,
dear readers,
could be more romantic
than all that?

Fist-Knock Future

They come back
the old machinists in their pickup trucks
bring back their rollaway toolboxes
full of wrenches forged before the Vietnam War
retired at age 67 or 68 they come back
at age 70 or 71 rolling their rollaway toolboxes
back across the concrete floor
the economic crash and their sons
and daughters they thought were gone for good
moved back into their houses
and their underwater houses and the high prices of medicine
forcing the old machinists back
through the tin door into the shop where they unpack
toolboxes and cover workbenches
with their measuring instruments they first held
when Mickey Mantle still gripped a Yankee bat
we talk
of all they know about milling machine feeds and speeds
and the spindle gears of old lathes
how good they are at putting a glass finish on steel
with their fingers and brains full
of 50 years of machine shop knowledge
then look
at their faces putting on brave 'good to be back' smiles
and see
the new lines on their foreheads
the skin sagging
under their jaws the hollow look
in their eyes
these men
who thought they had put in the years and fought the war
with the screaming
of drill bits and foremen
these men who thought they could finally put their feet up
for good

and lift grandchildren in their tired arms
and laugh back
tying the denim aprons around their waists
and stuffing earplugs into their ears again
but they will not let us feel sorry for them
as they straighten their backs
stick out their chins like they did
when they first picked up a micrometer
as The Beatles invaded America
and teenagers danced The Watusi
and smile across the sea of workbenches and belt sanders
and spinning lathe chucks
at the young machinists
so eager to learn
the young machinists
with their hip new beards and tattoos
and sides-of head-shaved haircuts
and fist-knocks and dreams
the old machinists
sidling up next to the young machinists
to show them a calculator
made the year *Light My Fire* was no. 1
a 12-inch Vernier calliper
made the year Nixon resigned a piece of paper
signed by the astronaut who first stepped on the moon
'Don't give up,'
their smiles say
'Don't give up your chance
to build a better world.'

No Room for Beethoven Kettle Drums

Sometimes for hours the tapping of a ball peen hammer
echoes between tin walls
a man
bent over stainless-steel tubes or titanium plates
he has machined
desperately tries
to hammer out dents in them
left by his bending or milling machine
his hammer blows exploding
like volcano blasts
or 4th of July cherry bombs
until someone across the factory picks up a copper hammer
and begins hammering
on a piece of steel trying to straighten it out
and there is a kind of hammer duet across hundreds of feet
of concrete shop floor
a duet chaotic
as Keystone cops shaking their batons at bank robbers
caws of angry crows on a telephone wire
the rattling of dice
in the fist of a crap shooter about to gamble away
his house
until
from somewhere in the factory comes a third hammer
a man beating out a rhythm on his sheet metal workbench
some jazz rhythm sweet as Charlie Parker or Dave Brubeck
or driving rock and roll like The Doors
he weaves
between the other hammer blows trying to turn chaos
into beauty
nervous energy
into inspiration
until men and women around the factory cock their ears
and put down their wrenches
and stare at him

in fear and disbelief
and after a minute or two
he stops
before a foreman comes barrelling out of a bullpen
and catches him
Keystone cops shaking their batons at bank robbers
or angry crow caws
or the rattling of dice in the fist of a man
about to lose
his house
are OK
but while a timeclock ticks
there is definitely no room in a factory
for music.

Timeless Wrench Brothers

Ismail the 19-year-old machinist puts his hands
on the handles of his machine
eager to learn
I look over
68 years old 44 years in the shops the paint
on the drawers of my toolbox
worn off by decades of my knuckles
opening and shutting the drawers searching
for ¼-20 bottom tap or 3/32 diameter drill
or 3-thousandths-of-an-inch-thick sheet metal shim
13 jobs
5 layoffs
dozens of bosses
under my belt
when I was Ismail's age a transistor radio
blasting The Doors' latest hit on a towel on a beach
was hi-tech
now his fingertip on his i-phone can choose
from millions of songs
but we both have hearts
and thumbs and doorknobs to turn and water to boil
and rays of dawn sun
falling through the high factory window
to warm our shoulders
at our machines on ice-cold 6am machine shop mornings
when I was 10 I hid under a school desk
doing duck-and-cover nuclear war drills
during the Cuban Missile Crisis
Ismail worries about chain saws
cutting down the Brazilian rain forests
when I was a boy Columbus was a god
now they are toppling his statue
in a park
Hemingway was kneeling on the African veldt
proud to shoot a charging lion

now the last lion may soon take its last step across this earth
but Ismail and I both grip wrenches and hammers
and dig our boots into concrete floor and drop vices
onto machine tables and laugh
in delight when a paycheque falls into our hands
Friday afternoon and know
when we see a coffin lowered into the ground
that life is short
we both have eardrums
and dreams and something inside us that will not let us sleep
when we have done wrong
when I was young robots were something we laughed at
in science fiction movies
now they may take
the wrench out of Ismael's hands
still
beer tastes as good on our tongues as it did
on Shakespeare's
wild horses still run down canyons under a full moon
the earth still turns
a woman still lets down her hair and saves a man's life
with her smile
still man stares up at a star and wonders
why
as he grabs a machine handle to make bolts that let
skyscrapers rise
toward the sky.

Timeclock Supermen

We once
thought we could be The Lone Ranger saving
people's lives and leaving silver bullets as we rode away
heroic with our masks on when we were 4
now we stand at machines
trying to get through another 10-hour day
heroic
if we can keep our chests stuck out like we will never crack
even though we are boring out our 10,000th identical
jackhammer casing
and want to scream
we know now at age 59 or 65 we will never be anything but
machinists
never leap a tall building in a single bound
shout a #1 punk rock song into a television hit parade
microphone
or invent a new kind of wrench
and retire to live the life of a playboy
in a dream house on a Hawaiian beach
we are a number
on a time-card
a face
interchangeable with millions of others
heading down a freeway toward some job
a fist
on a machine handle a heart
beating its 3 billionth beat
we are no longer the centre of the universe
shouting with joy blowing out a candle at our 1st birthday
party but aging machinists digging
our steel-toed shoes into a concrete floor
in front of an engine lathe or vertical mill
straining with everything we have inside us
to make it through another day
our heroic act

holding a grandson to our chest
like he will never have to want for love in this world
our mark
on history going on
setting feeds and speeds and calibrated dials
to make the wheels on streetcars
and the rods in car engines
shine
our Lindbergh crossing of the Atlantic
our Babe Ruth trot around the bases
our shot
heard round the world
just making it through that tin door one more day
tying on the leather apron
straightening our backs like no one on earth ever stood taller
sticking out our chins
and smiling one more time like there will never be anything
more special and irreplaceable
than a man
doing his best.

Not Everyone Can Have a Nervous Breakdown in the Middle of the Mojave Desert

At 67 I am finally nearing retirement age
not ready to retire yet
in the early morning dawn light I am ready
to open my car door
extra wide
I am ready
to not turn my stereo down as the door swings open wide
so the stereo's sound drifts across the company parking lot
to the ears of machinists and forklift drivers and deburrers
and solvent tank workers in straw hats
getting out of their cars
to go to work
for over 40 years I have hidden
my true identity as a poet
from my fellow workers
all the ideas I have for poems hidden
inside my head as I hammered on steel blocks
felt the air sucked out of my lungs by blast furnaces
and joked with men who read nothing
but muscle car magazines
afraid they might think I was gay or communist
or crazy and degenerate and not fit to work next to
but now
I have the Russian composer Stravinsky's 1952 Greek ballet
Agon playing on my stereo
written after he'd moved to L.A. and had a nervous breakdown
driving across the Mojave Desert
Agon is nothing but weird dissonant trumpet pops and bass
fiddle groans and kettle drum explosions and violin screeches
totally out of time
and without chords atonal and arhythmic sounding
as if a bomb
had dropped on an orchestra
and all that was left were insane traumatized musicians

playing shattered instruments
and I swing my car door all the way wide open
and turn Stravinsky up louder
as I swing my legs out my car door
and lace up my steel-toed boots
in 1913
Stravinsky's ballet *The Rite of Spring*
caused a riot in Paris
people screamed threw chairs tore out their hair
going into fits of rage over the weird sounds
they heard
one day
before I retire I wish I could find the courage
to climb up onto my steel workbench and read
some of my poems in booming unafraid voice
for all the workers
around me to hear
I may never cause a riot in Paris
or have a nervous breakdown
in the middle of the Mojave Desert
but at least I will have made a few waves
in a machine shop.

What is a Hammer Compared to the Heart of a Brother?

The white machinists lock up their tools
in their toolboxes each night
they etch their names with electric etching guns
into their wrenches and callipers
and micrometers and hammers and protractors
and lock them away
in their toolboxes each night with latches
and sometimes big heavy padlocks
and even chains
counting drills and chuck keys and cutting taps
with an eye always peeled
for thieves
they believe in jail cells electric chairs hellfire
loan nothing
and paste big stickers saying 'NO!'
to the insides of their toolbox lids
as the Mexican machinists hand each other their tools
with big smiles on their faces
leave their toolbox drawers open
and never lock their toolboxes
and sing
old socialist songs from the revolution south of the border
old mariachi love songs
their grandparents sing in old East L.A. houses
where 4 generations of their family
live together
sharing
everything
what is a wrench compared to the faith they have they will take care
of each other
what is a hammer compared to the heart
of a brother
what is a toolbox full of tools for

the seas
the moon
the rain that makes this earth green if not
us all
as rice is thrown at weddings and children kneel
at great grand parents' deathbeds
and crucifixes shine in the palms of old Mexican ladies
ready for heaven
as Emiliano Zapata's eyes burn
and Che Guevara camps in the hills
and the white machinists grow bitter
clutching their tools as their billionaires lock billions away
in bank vaults and the polar ice caps
melt and the land
they took from the Mexicans burns
in global warming drought
and the Mexicans smile handing each other their tools
and their hearts.

I Needed a Poem to Leap into My Brain and Bring Me a Woman

Nothing is lonelier than working in a factory Saturday night
with no woman
why
do gears turn cutting oils squirt the teeth of saws chew
if not for woman
why do we close micrometer anvil and barrel
around block of steel
and measure thickness to one ten thousandth of an inch
perfection if not for the beauty
of a woman's eyes
the warmth
of her breasts and arms pressed against us
and I hadn't had a woman in 8 years and the trains
brought the 1-ton steel bars
every Saturday night so the rolling overhead crane man
could roll them
to my blast furnace so I could hug them and shove them
toward roaring flame but why
do the panthers leap the fiddlers fiddle the fishermen pull fish
from the deep blue sea why
do hammers ring out forklifts lift cutting torches sizzle
shooting blue flame carving red-hot steel into bulldozer teeth
that will move
mountains
if not for the curve of the lips
of a woman
and what is lonelier than smokestacks above you belching
the orange and blue flames
of molten steel out of a tin roof Saturday night
when you haven't had
a woman in 8 years
why do train wheels roll
saxophones point toward the stars butterflies
flap blue wings tightrope walkers teeter rivers

carve canyons shoeshine men crouch over leather
last chance dreamers bet it all
and roll the dice
why are we out here on a shop floor Saturday night
with hardhats on and backs sweaty
when others
float in Venice gondolas or lean out over Rio de Janeiro cruise
ship rails and kiss women
in moonlight
why are wrenches gripped engines gunned battleships
launched
pool balls sunk dinosaur bones dug up telescopes focused
if not so a woman can take a man into her arms
and show him why
the sun still rises?

Trumpet Solo for Tomorrow

After 38 years in the machine shops I walk my tired bones
across the concrete floor and see
the new-hire lathe man
young
with a bounce in his step and a gleam in his eyes striding
toward his engine lathe
like the sky's the limit
after 35 years of unions busted
wages stalled
pensions gone houses lost healthcare crumbling bosses
screaming men
living under cardboard boxes in alleys who once had homes
for a minute I am surprised
there are still young men
like this new-hire reaching out to take the steel handles
of machines in their palms
and smile
but of course there are
of course
there are still meteors and baby feet taking their first steps
and leaps
of joy into the air and mountains to climb
and white-water rapids
to shoot canoes through and rake angles
on lathe cutting tools to grind to razor-sharp 7-degree
perfection and trumpet solos
to bring a tear to the eye and birthday cake candles
to raise a shriek of laughter in a 1-year-old girl
who can stop
the rose opening
the morning glowing
and suddenly my bones don't feel so tired
as long
as there are young men grabbing the handles to machines
there is a chance

to change the world
bring back the unions
give the men in cardboard boxes homes
put so much soul into carving a brass hub to a wheelchair
wheel on a machine no one
can tell you you are not
a hero
as someone hits the note on a trumpet
that will turn all our hearts
to gold
and we all grab the handles to our machines
like just when we thought it was so dark there was no longer a
shred of hope
it was really
the crack
of dawn.

Wasn't Columbus a Bachelor?

'If I had a couple million dollars I'd buy us tickets
to outer space!' Frank says
looking far out with sparkling eyes across the sea
to the moon over the horizon
as he and Jane walk the boardwalk in Long Beach
'What?!' Jane says
'You know. That billionaire that's building a shuttle
that will take a person to outer space
for a quarter million dollars
I'd buy 2 tickets!'
'WHY?!'
'Why?' Frank throws his arm out
toward the horizon Columbus sailed into
'Because you fly out past the atmosphere
and you're in outer space!
You experience weightlessness
you float around like those people in that movie *2001*
and then you look out a window and see the earth
so far away it's curved!'
'I don't like that movie', Jane says
'Outer space is boring. There's nothing there'
'But what an experience! What an adventure!
Wouldn't you like to defy gravity
and look back at the earth floating in the blackness
of outer space like a ball?'
'Weightlessness? Defying gravity? How would we pee?
We women would have to be catheterized
You men would have a little cup in your space suit'
'But what about the spectacular view of the curved green earth
out the window?
What about the beautiful sunrise?'
'But what about the glare.
They wouldn't let me wear my sunglasses
I'd get a migraine'
'But what about floating weightless

and leaving all your earthbound chains behind?'
'OK Carl Sagan! What would we eat?
Suck Spam out of a tube?
We couldn't drink any champagne or cognac
It would float away and get in my hair
and make it frizz!'
Frank looks up at the moon over the horizon again
and tries to concentrate
on the magic of the universe
and floating carefree and weightless in outer space
while gazing back
at the green earth's beautiful curved edge
and looks at Jane walking beside him happy
with her feet
firmly on the earth

Wasn't Columbus a bachelor?

Spark Spent: Mild-mannered Machinist

'Spark Spent'
Jane calls Frank
referring to the tired shy so-average-he's-boring never-reads-or-writes-anything persona
Frank adopts in the machine shop
Clark Kent rips off his dorky reporter clothes
in that phone booth
to reveal the big 'S' for Superman
on his chest
while Frank as Spark Spent comes home
from the machine shop to take off his stinky style-less
kryptonite-stained shirt and greasy jeans
and reveals on his chest
the big 'P'
for Poet Man
then takes a volume of Neruda or Whitman or Akhmatova or Shakespeare or Bukowski
off his shelf and throws it open and reads
poetry no one in the machine shop ever dreamed of
and takes pen
and sits down with soul as big as all the stars in the universe to write
a sizzling poem
Frank smiles
as the teeth on the cutter in his machine head make
a block of heat-treated steel
shudder and smoke
contemplating how boring and uninteresting
everyone in this machine shop thinks he is
because he has fooled them again with his mild-mannered
hugs-close-to-his-machine-all-day never-has-anything-to-say
Spark Spent act
as Jane
waits at home for him to burst through the door
and fly with his imagination about the room

on the wings of inspiration writing
his latest poem
that might change the world
as Poet Man
able to leap tall bookcases in a single bound
faster than a speeding metaphor
more powerful than a locomotive of stream of consciousness
up up and away
for Truth, Justice
and the Poetic Way.

Who Needs Relativity When You've Got Dumpsters?

A crow
lands on the telephone wire outside the big open tin door
as I pull the handle to a milling machine drilling
3/16th-inch diameter holes in titanium plates
then stop
to stare up at him
he half-flaps his wings ruffling and adjusting and refolding
them until they sit right
on his back like a man before a mirror shifting his body
about in a cheap black suit
trying to get it to hang right on his shoulders
this morning
instead of pulling a milling machine handle
maybe he is surveying this industrial area
for dead rats to eat
or maybe
he is just counting dumpsters with garbage in them
or enjoying
the sunrise like I am
I hear the crow is one of the most intelligent birds
and right now
he seems to have it on me as he holds his head up high
on that wire
and sticks his breast out and caws whenever he feels like it
over a thousand rooftops with no time clock
to punch or boss
to fear
his mind or soul may not stretch quite as far as Einstein's
or Buddha's but as he turns his head
and stares down at me I know that crow
wouldn't trade place with me
in a million years
he's hopping up and down on that wire with enthusiasm now
cawing and probably

laughing at me
he doesn't have to hold
a plus or minus 3-thousandths-of-an-inch
hole diameter tolerance all day
or wear a company shirt with his name on it
or smile at fellow workers
he'd like to punch in the nose
or pay taxes
or worry about identity theft or parts inspectors
or colonoscopies or bad breath or Alzheimer's
or parking tickets or atom bombs
or global warming or trying to get a raise
out of a tightwad boss
and if the polar ice caps melt
he'll just fly someplace cooler
and caw even louder.

Charles Bukowski's Groupie

After Frank and Jane have driven over the green Vincent
Thomas bridge from Long Beach
to San Pedro to go to Amalfitano's Bakery
for Frank's favourite chocolate/walnut fudgies
Jane tells Frank to drive by Charles Bukowski's house
driving down the hill with the port of L.A./Long Beach
red cranes in sight
Frank knows
the way by heart
'Look the trees have been pruned and you can see
the window of the room where Bukowski wrote!'
Jane says with delight
Jane has told Frank many times that Frank and Charles
Bukowski are her favourite poets
and Frank looks for a few moments at the window
where Charles Bukowski looked out
at the green bridge and the port's red cranes
and wrote
then Frank heads on down the street
'Let's go round the block and look at it again!
I want to feel Bukowki's spirit!' Jane says
Frank lowers his brow and frowns
'Why would I want to see it again?' he says
'Why would I want to be Charles Bukowski's groupie?!'
Frank steps down harder on the accelerator
Jane once knew Charles Bukowski
in one of his letters he asked her
to come do a Greek dance with him
in his new house on the hill
just because Charles Bukowski has sold thousands of times
more copies of his books
than Frank has
and had several major motion pictures made of his work
doesn't mean Frank should drive around the block
to look at his window again

Frank has his own window
where he writes and looks out at the next-door apartment
building's laundry room
and a red ACE HARDWARE trash can
and someday after he's dead he will be famous and people will
cruise down 2nd Street in Long Beach
and point it out
after the gardeners have pruned back the fig tree in front of it
but as Jane says, 'C'mon Frank!'
at the last moment Frank hits the brakes and jerks his arm
and turns his Toyota right at the intersection
and starts the drive around the block
like he has dozens of times before

Why be small?
He'll never be able to drive by his own window
after he's dead
and a magnificent view of the 40-ton cranes
in the largest port in the US
sure does beat an ACE HARDWARE
trashcan.

Art that Roars

Machinists tape paintings of their old classic cars
to their toolboxes and stare at them
like they were Picassos
lines of chrome side strips and bumpers and white roofs
and green hoods thrill
their hearts as they stand before them with fingers to chins
and deep thoughtful expressions on their faces
they drive
those old cars to work and gather round them
in the gravel parking lot at lunch
and let themselves feel the aesthetic pleasure
of how far apart and shiny their dual exhaust pipes
are how soft and well-stitched their red tuck and roll
upholstery is authentic
orange California license plates from the 1950s
are Cezanne peaches
thick un-dented chrome bumpers
gleaming in the hot L.A. noon sun
Van Gogh sunflowers
as they walk around those cars and peer in their windows
and ooh and aah
like those art lovers
they'd always made fun of in High School
4-on-the-floor gear shifts
and tachometers and speedometers that go to 130mph
in Mustangs and T-Birds
where beautiful women cross their legs
beside them is their idea of a Mona Lisa
worth ogling
they can stop
slapping and punching and poking each other and fall in love
with these cars
they have restored with a touch as delicate
as Michelangelo's
cars that can roar

and shoot gravel and speed out of that parking lot
after the quit-work whistle blows
deadly
as rattlesnakes
and as the steel mill smokestack belches
red-hot stinking orange sparks
the machinists step up to those cars and stroke them
unashamed
to fall in love with art that can go from 0 to 60mph
in 7 seconds.

A Thousand Secrets of Steel in His Fingers

When I was young and learning to be a machinist
I'd be hired
at a company and roll my toolbox on a cart down an aisle
to a machine
Bridgeport
or Cincinnati vertical mill
or maybe even a Polish horizontal mill with a name
I'd never heard of before
strange knobs and gear shifts and ancient gear belts
and automatic feed levers
to the machine table's 'x' and 'y' axes
even 'Machine Start' buttons I couldn't find
puzzled me
a block of steel that had to be turned into a part per a
blueprint
in front of me
a roof over my head and the bread on my table
at stake
as machinist veterans who knew the machines backwards
and could make them do anything
watched me
out of the corners of their eyes and stayed silent
and kept the secrets of sine bars and trigonometry tables
and universal heads
and spindle speeds and red-hot chips and steel screams
to themselves
until an old machinist with a thousand secrets of steel
in his fingers would finally walk over
and show me the handles I needed to throw
the stub drill
I needed to lock into the Jacobs chuck
the set-up with nuts and bolts and clamps I needed to make
on the machine table to machine the part
an old machinist
who remembered what it was like to wake up in the morning

and not know
if you could make your way
in this world
who hadn't become as hard
as crowbars and ballpeen hammers and concrete floors
and tin walls
and razor-sharp tool steel cutters and foremen and companies
who worshipped dog-eat-dog bottom lines
a machinist
who knew there was nothing in this world
more important
than a flesh and blood
helping hand.

Steel-Toed Soul

When I was twelve I wore brown wing-tip shoes
to church
where they said Jesus rose again from the dead
now I wear steel-toed boots
to work in a machine shop where heaven
is a quit-work whistle sending us machinists out the door
with paycheques
to be born again under a blue sky
once my 12-year-old neck chafed in summer heat
under a starched white collar
as I knelt before the altar and sipped
the blood of Christ in burgundy wine and tasted
his body wafer-thin on my tongue
now
blood flows from my fingers sliced by razor-sharp cutters
as I sweat
in torn T-shirt slicing steel into parts
so the boss doesn't send me to the street
where I could starve
a bird on a telephone wire
outside the tin door of the factory
sings to my 63-year-old soul when once
I held a hymnal as my first beard sprouted on my chin
and I sang
about the blessings of God
college
and my clean hands on a scalpel or a law book
or around a university lectern and all the success in the world
lay ahead for me
now I lace up my steel-toed boots
and grip a tool steel wrench in my dirty fist
and think of those brown wing-tip shoes I once wore
when Jesus rose
from the dead each Easter
and go on

carving my living out of cutting steel real
as this hard hard world
and finding what blessings I can
in these poems.

A Planet I Never Learned About in Any Book

Going to school growing into a man I learned
there had been world wars
there was something called the subconscious
Poe
died in a Baltimore gutter
I never learned there were men with faces toughened
and tanned as leather
from standing in front of white-hot blast furnace flames
all their lives
I learned
the universe began with a big bang 13.5 billion years ago
things are made of atoms and men go insane
from sniffing paint thinner
on prison rooftops but no one told me about men
who could make the same motorcycle valve all day
in the corner of a roaring sunless factory
for 20 years
and still laugh like there was nothing better
than being alive
I knew
about the rings of Saturn and Cary Grant taking LSD
and 6 million Jews
dying in Nazi concentration camps
but never
how lonely and unknown a man could feel trapped between
windowless factory tin walls working his life away
I'd taken tours of colleges
sipped the blood of Christ from chalices
in the hands of ministers in front of altars
seen the burned tiles on the bottom of an astronaut's capsule
just back
from outer space
but never knew
a man with a wrench or a welding rod
or a micrometer in his hand

could put as much heart and soul into his work as any artist
who ever hung a painting
in the Louvre
and at age 22
I dropped out of PhD school in English literature
and walked into a steel mill
like stepping
onto another planet
saw creatures
in hardhats and steel-toed boots I stared at like they were
strange animals behind bars
in a zoo
working men
no one had told me about back in school
working men
it would take me dozens of years to learn
were my brothers.

Psychopaths Give Good Interviews

'Warning: This machine can cause Serious Injury or Death,'
the machines say in bold letters
permanently glued to their sides
but there are no warning tags glued to the sides
of machinists
the company gives talks to us machinists on what to do
if a magnesium or titanium fire breaks out
or someone catches their hand in a machine
but they give us no guidelines
for discerning when we are working next to a psychopath
and what to do about it
I have had to somehow keep my cool
when the nightshift operator of my machine
who had made bombs in the Korean army
left a perfect facsimile of a hand grenade in clay
on top of my toolbox to warn me
to work slower
somehow figure out
how to humour and cajole the speed freak machinist
at the mill next to mine
who kept laughing as he threatened to meet me
in the parking lot with a knife
I never got a raise for enduring such machinists
supervisors shake their heads and walk away
when you try to tell them
Herman at the next machine thinks aliens
hovering in a spaceship above the factory roof
are speaking to him through a chip
they've planted in his brain
I have worked next to a man
who blasted an Oldies but Goodies radio station
into my ears for years
and managed not to kill him
had to tell
an ex-gang member lathe operator to fuck off

so he'd leave me alone when I'd feared
he'd pull a gun from his toolbox
the employee manual doesn't cover such things
psychopaths are good
at getting hired by giving interviews
that make them look like model employees
and you walk out on a concrete shop floor and wonder
if the next man you work near
will make headlines by pulling out a machine gun
and going on a bloody
workplace rampage or just slowly drive you mad
by gradually uncovering all your weak spots
and gleefully sticking needles
into them
machines with steady gears and droning heads
and relentless grinding cutters may be boring
but machinists
never are.

One Man Zoo

'It would be easier to teach a gorilla
to do my Federal Income Tax Return
than to teach you to clean our kitchen,'
Jane tells Frank
and Frank is about to get mad but then thinks
what a wonderful gift Jane has with hyperbole.
'It would be easier to put panty hose on a giraffe
than get you to wear a shirt and pants that match!'
Jane tells Frank
and Frank knows there can't be many men on this earth
who ever get compared to a giraffe in panty hose
by a wife so gifted
in spectacular analogy.
'You rattle those beads louder
than a psychotic rhinoceros Frank!'
Jane groans to Frank
covering her ears after Frank puts his head down
and charges for the thousandth time
through the wooden-bead curtain in the doorway
to their bedroom
making it crackle like gunfire
and Frank smiles.
Other wives might compare their husbands
to pro football players
or Hulk Hogan or a bull in a china shop
but only Jane could refer to *Rhinoceros*
that theatre of the absurd play by Eugene Ionesco
Frank has read 6 or 7 times
where a big rhinoceros charges through a small European
village over and over
and tramples people as 2 villagers argue
about whether it has 1 horn or 2
and even though Frank knows
the rhinoceros in Ionesco's play is a symbol for Nazism
and Frank certainly doesn't want to really trample anybody

it is kind of fun for Frank to have a wife
so clever at literary allusion
she can have Frank playing the title role
in one of Frank's favourite plays
while she insults him.

If a man has to be nagged
at least he should be nagged by a wife
with imagination.

Solidarity in Hard Times

One Sunday morning when Frank and Jane are having tea
and Frank is feeling
especially noble recalling his days in the steel mill he says,
'I used to shove 30 tons of steel a week
into the mouth of a white-hot blast furnace....'
waiting for Jane to nod in awe
and sympathy but Jane recalling her days in the go-go bars
says,
'I used to carry 4 pitchers of beer in each hand
all night serving the drunks....'
'The 2-ton drop hammers used to smash down on the
concrete floor so hard
it quaked like an earthquake and I could barely walk
and my stomach rose
and my heart leaped...'
Frank goes on
waiting for Jane to realize the immense ordeal he has endured
and survived
but Jane says, 'My legs were so tired after serving beer
and go-go dancing
for 10 hours with no break
I had to crawl up the stairs to my bedroom at the end
of the night....'
Frank grips his teacup as hard as a sledgehammer
and sticks out his jaw and says,
'The drills and the air compressors and the furnaces
and the drop hammers
were so loud men who worked that steel mill 20 years
shook constantly
in their fingers and jaws....'

But Jane fires back,
'Those rock bands were so loud I couldn't hear for an hour
after I left work.'
Frank is about to slam his teacup down when he stops
and realizes
Jane's bosses screamed at her
just as much as his bosses ever screamed at him
he realizes
he's been stared at
by drugged-out knife-carrying biker machinists
but Jane had drunken crazy men leer
and flirt with her bikini fringe
for years
he can't win
and Frank gives up and moves over in bed
and snuggles up to Jane and puts his arm around her
while contentedly sipping hot Earl Grey tea and says,
'We've had it pretty rough,'
and smiles.

In America the unions might be busted
and socialism a dirty word
but at least Frank gets to be married
to a beautiful
comrade in arms.

Beautiful as a Picket Line Under a Rising Sun

'Beautiful!'
my Lead Man would exclaim as he held an aircraft part
I'd cut out of aluminium
up into the light of the 10,000-Watt bulbs shining down
from the 70-foot-high machine shop ceiling
and it *was* beautiful
in those days of the unions
decades ago
my Lead Man's ex-hippie long hair
tied in a pony tail hanging down his back
beautiful
as our union wages that paid for houses and boats
and college educations for our children
and vacations to Europe and the pensions solid as a rock
we looked forward to
and the health care we could count on to carry us through
heart attack
or cancer
beautiful
as the muscle and pride of Gus the 40-year-veteran bedmill
operator who walked
the concrete floor around his machine
like a lion
making mountains of steel and aluminium chips
no man could match
so he could ride home on his full-dresser Gold Wing
motorcycle shaking his long hair
in the wind
and laugh
'Right On!'
our Lead Man would yell like a Black Panther freedom
marcher in 1969 asserting his right to be
a human being
when he picked up and admired an aircraft part we'd cut as we
machinists

looked at each other and smiled
strong as a union picket line
under a rising sun
a brotherhood
solid as a 30-pound tool steel cutter carving titanium
into an airplane wing carry-through section
sure as a 7-foot-long boring bar shaving a hole
through a big-as-a-car landing gear
that would let an airplane carrying 300 people
land
soft as a good dream on a goose-down pillow
we were right on
and beautiful
as Martin Luther King and Bobby Kennedy before they were
shot
a machinist
with a union card in his pocket letting him walk so tall
no boss
could ever stare him down
an aircraft wing actuator we'd machined
sitting shining and perfect in our palm
a grandson
we'd lifted into our arms smiling up at us
because he knew
we'd always leave him
a better world.

The Universe Can't Stop Laughing

We are the steel I-beam spines
of cities
the nails holding together the house where Mark Twain lay
dying under Halley's Comet
the pawnbroker
sad
holding a dented trumpet he's sure could have blown a note
so strong
it made the sunrise brighter the polisher
of faucets full of cold water in a green-tinted train station
washroom dreaming
of his dead wife's kiss the hand
gripping the trapeze bar 100 feet above a circus tent
dirt floor as a thousand people gasp below the fingers
of a mechanic full of lube grease that let the wheels
of a Volkswagen bus painted a hundred colours roll across
the Golden Gate Bridge
during San Francisco's summer of love
we are paintbrush
hair clippers channel-lock pliers 80-grade sandpaper
butcher's scale table saw blade watchmaker eyeball streetcar
conductor thumb
lion tamer sweat axle grease
on a cheek popcorn bag at a baseball game
chess piece in a park Hitler in a barber chair bolt thread
and blowtorch we are
shoemaker for mad King George chauffeur
for drunk Jim Morrison fingernail clipper
for the stars stirrer
of paint eater
of fire
we raced locomotives across the American frontier
like God told us to
ran out of gas halfway to Vegas
we are hubcap

and scalpel vaccine
and sword swallower toothpick factory
and birdwatcher
straightjacket and rocket launch stopwatch setter
and card casino royal flush chainsaw teeth sharpener
and nitro-glycerine hugger atom splitter
and eclipse watcher
Death Row harmonica
and Wright Brothers glider Edgar Allen Poe orangutan
and Gypsy Rose Lee G-string front row ticket
to the end of the world and Albert Einstein's
worst haircut as we stand in line
to punch a timeclock and the universe
can't stop
laughing.

Jim Morrison Thumbs a Ride on 4th Street

On mornings like this as I drive toward work at 6.21am
4th Street stretches ahead
without end
as I stick my arm out my window and roll back
my sunroof as the sky begins to lighten
my long-dead father
waves to me from a barber chair
as the red white and blue pole spins
ready to tell me never-before-told stories
of riding boxcars in the depression
the man
in the donut shop window waving his arms with wild eyes
delivering a speech
to the rest of the donut munchers knows the secret
to world peace
Jim Morrison
didn't die but is a minor aging poet with long grey hair
walking to a beat in his head
he wants me to get him a reading
at the Long Beach Poetry Festival
he sticks out his thumb and I wave at him but keep on rolling
because I will always
have my chances to stop and give him a ride and listen to him
audition
Charlie Chaplin twirling his cane as he waits at a bus stop
a whiff
of albondigas soup from the red brick Honduras Kitchen
Buddhists
in orange robes leaving the monastery to walk down sidewalks
and see
gas stations and old men walking dogs in the sunrise
Charlie Parker
standing on a corner kicking the heroin and booze for good
with a cup of black coffee
in his fist

and the next great jazz breakthrough
in his head
I could ride 4th Street forever
but I turn and head for the freeway
to roll into work
on a morning like this I am not just another factory worker
but the only machinist poet on earth
the one no High School
or university or job ad ever
predicted
and there is nothing on earth I would rather do
than pick up a wrench
and wonder who
will step out of the shadows to stroll down 4th Street
tomorrow.

Ready to Go to Work

A machinist bites into his morning apple
as the sun rises
on his workbench before him are 1/8th to ½-inch Allen wrenches
for turning socket-head cap screws
tight
5/16th to 1-and-¼-inch crescent wrenches
for turning any hex-nut
in the shop
and the apple in his mouth is sweet as its juice drips
from his lips to the concrete floor
and he knows
he can do anything with his tools
as birds chirp on a telephone wire and asteroids float
in outer space
why can't politics
be as cut and dried
as the calibration marks on his machine dials
nuclear test-ban treaties negotiated
as easily as he can indicate a vice parallel
on his machine table
parts
for ships rockets tubas fire hydrants microscopes elevators
toasters and skyscrapers can be made
on the lathes and mills and surface grinders
around this machine shop
and with the morning kiss of his wife
and the photo of his granddaughter taped
to the inside of his toolbox lid
the machinist strides like the black panther
stands poised
over his vice like a heron hunting
over a pool of water
a hundred meteors striking the earth one billion years ago
in the block of steel

he is about to cut
the apple
that made Newton see gravity stretched to the stars
in his hand
the machinist takes his last bite of the apple
and tosses the core into a trash can and wonders
why can't
all the children starving in this world be fed
all the homeless
standing on street corners housed all the oceans cleaned
all the lights turned on
by windmills
and the machinist rolls his thumb across the worm screw
in his red adjustable crescent wrench
and fits its jaws around a big hex-nut and wishes
someone would give him the blueprint
so he could make
a better world.

Turning Dillinger into Shakespeare

When I stepped into that steel mill I felt
like a criminal
murdering everything I had been brought up to believe in
the white shirt
the polished shoe clean fingernails cross of Jesus
above a communion cup
full of his blood
that would save me
in the steel mill blood was something that spurted
from a finger cut off by a saw blade
eternity
a 12-hour shift heaven
a quart schooner of frothy beer poured across the lips
I'd never looked into the eye of a steel cutter
or a 10-ton overhead crane
or Wheel-A-Brator deburring machine operator
in my life
but I would look deeply into the eyes of these men
if it killed me
and I would never wear a white shirt
never lecture on Shakespeare or Shelley
from a university podium
belong to bridge club
or yacht club
or look down my nose at any man on the face of this earth
again
I would learn
what made the lion roar
gold shine a wave
roll a rose open in the hand of a girl in love with a machinist
a panther step
under a midnight moon a mustang shake its mane
and gallop
toward a horizon I would heat
steel red-hot at the mouth of a roaring blast furnace

and look into the eyes of these men and learn
what made Van Gogh splash stars across a canvas
Joe Louis punch Hitler in the eye the whale leap
for the sun eggs sizzle on sidewalks Mr. Bojangles dance
till he floats Halley's Comet
spread its tail each snowflake
unique each smile from the heart
holy I would lift tons and tons of steel in my arms
and look into their eyes and learn
what makes a diamond sparkle a Monarch butterfly
flap its wings
sitting high up on a redwood tree needle in the sun
I would look
into the eyes of those men and learn
that instead of being a criminal I was
a poet.

Laughter Lifeboat

In a machine shop a machinist will laugh
whenever he can
no matter how dirty or tired he is
no matter how many tiny stainless-steel slivers he can't see are stabbing
his palms
no matter how many years it's been since he's gotten a raise
he will laugh
whenever he can
it is his last weapon
after all the layoffs
toothaches wage cuts crazy bosses
raised rents freeway tire blowouts
near mental crackups near gunfire near suicide
after his wife has left him for the vice president
of a bag company
and he has broken his last shoelace rather
than break down crying or go berserk and punch out his boss
he will think
of something funny
and tell other machinists near him about it
and they will all begin laughing louder and louder
until all the machinists
in the area at their workbenches and machines are laughing
and the laughter becomes a lifeboat
and everyone climbs in
and keep it floating
by laughing
aching machinists with arthritis and hernias and bad backs
sad machinists whose wives left them for plumbers
or stockbrokers
bored machinists who don't know if they can stand watching
their fly-cutter shave steel
one more minute
without going mad

machinists with bad knees bad landlords bad consciences
bad brakes bad bets bad credit
bad haircuts laugh until the tears roll down their cheeks
and their bodies shake from head to toe
laughter is all they have left
and it is warm in their belly and soothing to their brain
and if they read
Camus
they might even know that they are probably
without knowing it also laughing
at the existential absurdity
of being the only creature on earth who knows
it must die
but right now it is enough to put down their wrenches
and hammers
and float
in the wonderful lifeboat
laughter.

Star-Spangled Purple Bandana General

When I first stepped up to a machine after getting
my union card
I joined a ring of men and women locking hands in a circle
spanning the globe
an army
with wrenches and hammers and steel-toed shoes and
hardhats and tape measures
instead of guns
an army standing so tall no CEO or supervisor
could stare us down
and when I picked up a wrench it was because
I really wanted
to pick up a wrench
we were rise
of mountain beat
of eagle wing beauty
of rose inevitable as wave crossing ocean to crash
into rock true
as gravity indispensable
as sunlight
Gus
in his Greek fisherman hat and black leather jacket cranking
the handle of his bedmill and smiling
Marcella
with her star-spangled purple bandana around her forehead
and her wrapped-in-green-surgical-tape fingers scraping
against her spinning buffing wheel
our generals
we were swing of miner's pick
deep in the copper mine in Chile the clipper ship seaman
high in his crow's nest bearing the frigid blast
of Cape Horn gale-force wind against his face the chef
over his steaming pot of clam chowder in his tall white hat
the San Francisco conductor
with his fist on his stick-shift changing screeching gears

on his cable car
crawling up the hill hamburger flipper
jackhammer gripper cathedral bell
ringer dynamite lighter railroad
switchman chimney sweeper
crawling-under-the-foundation-of-the-house
plumber Brazilian Grand Opera singer
and Paris piano tuner
and I stood at my machine and looked out a tin door
as the sun rose
over the San Gabriel mountains
as a jeweller cut a priceless diamond
and a janitor polished a train station washroom faucet
and felt the warmth of the blood flowing in our locked hands
circling the globe
our globe
our home
our brotherhood/sisterhood
lighting up our sky
of dreams.

Grow Back Green

At 3am
there is nothing lonelier than a blast furnace flame
and the young man
shoving 1-ton steel bars into its mouth dreaming
of the woman he cannot find
because he must work nights
train horns
2-ton drop hammers pounding
orange flames shooting out of factory roof smokestacks
seem about to wake the dead
at 3am
as the young man hangs onto a rake stirring a molten lake
of red-hot steel
and 10,000-watt light bulbs
glare from the ceiling between tin walls
and he feels 10,000 miles away
from a soft bed
outside
the tin walls on break he stares up at the moon
and stars as cats
and cockroaches hunt
the electric streetlights of the L.A. basin stretched out
around him
in the blackness
something in him longs
for all the lights to be turned out
all the trucks and trains
parked
the drills and reamers and rivet guns and furnaces stopped
the televisions and radios and computers
switched off
so that men in the darkness and silence may learn
to truly dream
again
dream

of a planet where the factories sit still all night
so the earth can begin to grow back
green.

Janis Joplin Never Belted Southern Comfort Bourbon and Screamed the Blues

'We've got to wear these fricking masks!'
says our new supervisor
to us machinists and de-burrers and shipping clerks
and punch press operators gathered
around him on the shop floor for the special coronavirus
pandemic meeting he has called
to tell us we must all wear our sanitary masks at all times
he says 'fricking'
instead of 'fucking'
because long since the days when he was a hippie
and said 'fucking' in every other sentence
he quit drugs
and drinking and blasting iconoclastic long-haired-hippie
rock music and joined
a fundamentalist Christian church
and started saying 'fricking' instead of 'fucking'
'fucking'
sounds earthy and solid and true and sexy and noble
as an elephant trumpeting
a steamroller rolling
a Hula dancer swaying her hips under a Waikiki palm tree
Freud uncovering a repressed memory
Joe Louis landing a KO punch to Max Schmeling's Nazi jaw
'fricking'
sounds like something that would make Jimi Hendrix
unplug his electric guitar
Romeo forget Juliet Harry Houdini
resign himself to handcuffs Valentino take off his tango shoes
Jim Morrison
put on a hair shirt
and the supervisor finishes by telling us to all wear our masks
at all times and stay
in good health and then shouts,
'Alright! Let's all get back to fricking work!'

would Paul Bunyan
have said 'fricking'
would that speeding locomotive driver Casey Jones
would Jack Dempsey Pablo Picasso
Janis Joplin never belted Southern Comfort bourbon
and screamed the blues
Leadbelly never split a chain-gang boulder
with a sledgehammer
and we machinists and shipping clerks and de-burrers
and punch press operators
file back toward our machines
as all the air goes out of all the balloons
on earth

Something like a pandemic that's a matter of global life
and death
ought to at least make men give
a fuck.

Sure and Solid as Einstein

There are old machinists
so good at their trade it seems astrophysicists
and archaeologists might
be humbled
these machinists sit on stools like Buddha
before their machines
with so much Zen-like
concentration in their eyes you'd swear they could smell
the black cutting oil on a 3/8th-16 tap
in a tooling cabinet 20 feet away
recite
the 4-foot-tall drill charts hanging on the tin walls listing
hundreds
of drill and reamer dimensions down
to one ten thousandth of an inch diameter
perfectly
as Lawrence Olivier doing his 'To Be or Not To Be'
Hamlet speech
spot
the difference between a .249 and a .250-inch-in-diameter
check pin
with their naked eye
feel
the head of their machine with their palm
and know how many days it has left
before a bearing cracks
stand the bare factory tin walls staring back at them
for 50 years
their jaw sure and solid as Einstein's
when he first wrote down
$E=mc^2$
to see them tie a lace on their steel-toed boot
or slip a 6-inch tool steel scale
into their leather apron's breast pocket is to watch
Michelangelo grip hammer and chisel

Lindberg stay awake all night in his tiny bi-plane
hanging over the Atlantic
Ulysses steer his boat Calypso through the wild waves between
the sharp edges
of the giant rock Scylla and the whirlpool Charybdis
Rembrandt should have painted these master machinists Lincoln
written a second Gettysburg address in their honour
boring half a thousandth of an inch off the walls of holes through
$30,000 aircraft parts they never scrap
with fingertips cool and steady as brain surgeon
or nitro-glycerine handler
they can mix a thousand machine head spindle speeds
and machine table feeds to make any metal
you ask them to cut
shine like glass
all they ask
is a sun in the sky a wave in the sea a curl
in the hair and a laugh on the lips
of a woman in their arms
and the mile-deep peaceful sleep of a man
who has spent a lifetime doing his job
well.

He Will Make Steel Sing

Told
to go to the back of the factory onto the engine lathe
he has never seen
or run the machinist stands
before all of the lathe's handles and set screws and speed settings and chucks
that could leave him helpless
and without a job in this factory where he has only worked for a month
he forces the panic
over all the things he doesn't understand about this machine
back down
inside himself
and spends 10 minutes searching for the power button
and finds it
and punches it and hears the engine start humming
as 20 years of machinist experience tell him to stay calm
calm as the lion
on the African grass where it has belonged
for millions of years
calm as the stars
that return each night like there is nowhere else they could ever have been
calm
as reason
that invented fire and time and gravity
as he moves to the silvery smooth handles
in front of the lathe's shiny tool steel ways
and with fingers tries each one
this way and that and this way and that for half an hour
until he throws the one
that starts the chuck spinning smoothly at 600 rpm
and suddenly he knows
that it will all fall into place
as surely as each moment will pass

each
handle each set screw each cutting tool will one by one
sooner or later make sense
and he will be able to go on feeding his family
because he will lean over this machine and turn wrenches
and throw its handles
cutting
steel part
after steel part after steel part more and more smoothly until
they sing
proving
once again that it isn't the machine
that made man but man
who made
the machine.

Champions

It is 98 degrees inside this tin building and I sit
on a stool
like a boxer in his corner between rounds near the end
of a long
long fight
40 years
in the machine shops with the heat and the sweat
and the foremen and the machines
and the deadlines
and I am 65 years old today and I am tired after 9 and ½ hours
on this concrete floor I feel
in every one of my bones
it is hard to get up from this stool
and drop my 94th aircraft part of the day into the vice
on the machine table and set the machine
cutting again
but Joe Louis got up
from his stool when the bell rang and he was old and tired
and could barely make it
through the 15th round
John Garfield got up
and went on acting in his last movie
as the House Un-American Activities Committee
turned the screws on him calling him a communist to wreck
his career
and his heart gave out
every man in this shop
gets up
from his stool as his bones ache and the foremen scream
and the raises never come
and the timeclock ticks
away his life
Siegfried
slayed the dragon Columbus dared drop off the edge
of the world

I write this poem
because someone has to tell the story of these men
who never stop getting up
from their stool to go to their machine as they grow old
making this world
out of steel and aluminium
at 62 or 65 or 75 years of age
maybe grandchildren or great grandchildren depend on them
maybe they just go on
because it's what they do
but as the heat rises and the foremen scream and the machines pound and grind
that bell rings in their hearts
and they gather all the strength left inside them
and get up
from their stools one more time
because that is what champions
do.

Robots Have No Bones

Old men
run the manual machines in this machine shop
I left the manual machines
and learned to run computer-controlled machines
so I'd be skilled on the cutting edge of technology
in case I got laid off
and needed to find another job
but as I grow old I miss running those old machines
feeling
their handles in my palm their vibrating tool steel tables
against my thighs the smell
of their grease-blackened worm screws the trembling
of the steel blocks in their vices deep in my bones as I strained
every muscle in my body leaning on those handles moving
cutters
through groaning steel
they say another wave of automation is coming
truck drivers
welders
rivetters
assemblers
machinists
replaced
by robots
and I stand at my computer machine
clicking through its automatic motions without me
and I look over at those men with their warm hands
around the handles of the manual machines
it felt good
feeling the trembling of steel in my bones as I gripped
a machine handle and carved the steel down
into axle
so a car could roll a just-married couple laughing
toward their honeymoon
a brass oxygen valve block

so a deep sea diver could look at blue coral for half an hour
deep
beneath the waves
it felt good
to feel the steel of skyscrapers bridges fire hydrants
jackhammers emergency ward door hinges
bulldozer teeth cane tips water faucets in my bones
as I made this world
it felt good
putting every muscle in my body into cutting valves
for pipes so water could flow down the
parched throats
of children
the hub
of a wheelchair wheel so a painter could roll to a window
and put his last sunset
on canvas
and what will we have left
after the computers and the robots have taken over
and we pace in circles flexing
our useless hands
what will we have left
when we can no longer feel this world
in our bones
and hearts?

As Close as it Gets

A critic in England said I wrote too many poems
about feeling guilty
about making parts for Air Force planes
that drop bombs
in Iraq
and even as I pick up the parts I have cut for fighter jets
and wipe the oily coolant off them and pack them away
I try to think
how far away the little girl who may be killed
by one of those bombs
is
two continents and a great ocean
and a vast world I didn't create and cannot control
between us
but then
cannot help seeing the sunlight on the red brick wall
outside the factory door
the same sunlight
right now in the hair of that little girl
as she skips down a sidewalk
and she is not far away at all
she is as close
as the air we both breathe
the star
we stare up at
and the rose we pick
to know how big and beautiful this universe
really is
she is as close
as the rain drop giving life to the blade of grass
my father lifting me onto his shoulder so I could
see the fireworks
when I was three
every shout of joy of every child who ever kicked a ball
in the street

every beat of my heart that would not want to live
without love
every lick
of the tongues of the cats in the street as an old man
from the factory next door comes out
to feed them his bowls
of soup
and as I wipe the green coolant off another of the fighter jet
parts with a shop rag
and pack it away
all I can say to that critic is
I tried
I tried to put some distance between myself and that little girl
but then found out
she was mine.

Cary Grant

Frank
stands before Jane's full-length antique armoire mirror even though he knows
no machinist within a hundred-mile radius
would ever stand before a mirror studying himself
in his clothes
the way she is having him do.
Jane
tugs on the hem and flaps and adjusts the lapels
of the fine used Armani suit she has bought him
from the vintage clothes store for $10
spreads
and adjusts Frank's hair on top to the collar
has him turn to the left then the right.
'Now you look good, Frank.
Now you look like a male model.'
He stares
at himself in the high-class black coat and pants
and longs for the machine shop
where his old streaked-with-grease blue jeans
droop down on his ass
and his baggy smelly style-less T-shirt
hangs on him like a tent
and he never looks at himself in the mirror at all
except to check
how big his beer belly is.
'You look better than Cary Grant.'
'Cary Grant?'
he shouts
resisting the urge to rip the coat off himself
and tear it to shreds.
'Why the fuck would I want to look better than Cary Grant?!'

Jane steps back
remembering that Frank
has only been away from the machine shop for a day
and she may be pushing him too hard.

The last thing a man
surrounded all day by grunting horny bestial men
only one step up from County Jail
wants to do
is look better than Cary Grant.

Always Ready to Grate Carrots

'I'm always ready to grate carrots!'
Frank shouts
in response to Jane's request for grated carrots
so she can make her famous carrot cake
though at the moment
Frank is reading *Beowulf* for the 3rd time out
on his balcony in the sun
and doesn't get up.
'I'm always ready to take out the trash, you know that!'
Frank shouts
after Jane drags out 2 big TRADER JOE'S bags full of garbage
though at the moment
he is sitting cross-legged on the floor in Buddhist meditation
and doesn't get up
because he is ready to enter Nirvana
where he knows a man is capable
of anything.
'I'm always ready to vacuum the living room rug!'
Frank shouts
after Jane opens the blinds to let the sun
shine in on their living room rug and points out
the mountains of throat-choking hair and dust balls rising up
all over it after months
and months of not being vacuumed
though at the moment
Frank is reading one of his own poems
about the joys of getting up in the morning knowing
you can do anything
and can't be bothered to get up.

When a man is as absolutely certain as Frank is
that he can do anything
what need is there to do
anything?

The Line No-one Crosses

It may be a comb
a man flourishes and waves above his head
and then runs through his hair
to give it that perfect wave before he clocks out
after another 10 hours on the machine
or
a pair of snakeskin boots the Black
man at the steel-part-cleaning tub of solvent wears
and keeps spotlessly clean all day amid the grease
and grime of the factory,
the picture of a dead wife on the inside of a toolbox lid
or the punch
through the air of a hand than once won a Golden gloves
championship,
the warble
in a machine shop washroom stall of a voice
that once recorded a record in Nashville
or the patch
of some long-defunct 60s outlaw motorcycle club
on the sleeveless Levi jacket
of an old man on a drill press,
but whatever it is
machinists stand back
in dread respect and without one trace of laughter
leave it well enough
alone
knowing
that even men
barely getting by on $10-an-hour on oily stinking machines
must have something sacred
they will fight to the death
for.

What Good is Gravity Without a Woman?

Working night shift in a factory and not having a woman
in 3 years is knowing how cold
a block of steel in your hands can be
at 10 minutes to midnight
how sharp
edges of tool steel cutters can slice through your heart
as they chew
groaning bronze
working night shift in a steel mill not having a woman
in 3 years is sitting
next to Vincent Van Gogh in a dive bar as he nods out
drinking green absinthe
because he knows no woman will ever
love him
it is sitting in a cell on death row hearing the horn of the train
carrying newlyweds toward their honeymoon
where they will swing from chandeliers
next to Niagara Falls
it is forgetting
why the rose blooms and men carrying lunch pails
in their fists stride into factories
and drop time cards into time clocks at 6am
like they can't wait
to feel white-hot blast furnace flames
sear the inside of their nostrils and laugh
because they have their women
it is sitting in a factory on Mars
as stinking coolant pours over smoking steel
in front of your face and lovers
sailing on cruise ships on Earth pop champagne corks
and make love
it is a Bengal tiger pacing
a 10-foot-wide cage
it is staggering outside tin walls at break
to stare at the full moon and wonder

how lovers wrapping their arms around each other floating
down Venice canals in gondolas
feel
it is lying awake unable to sleep in a lonely dusty bed knowing
the only thing in the world
you have to hug is a filthy 1-ton bar
of steel
it is a cat without a meow
a Santa without a sleigh bell
a solar system without a sun
Beethoven shaking his fist at God
Galileo
walking back down the steps of the Leaning Tower of Pisa
not having dropped
those 2 cannonballs of different size and weight
because he no longer cares
what gravity is.

Gas Pumps and Metal Legs

At the intersection I wait in the 5.21am darkness
Shell gas station and convenience store on one side
Veterans Affairs hospital on the other
2 young veterans of the Iraq war are crossing the street
in front of my car
on those metal sticks
they give them for legs
after their real ones have been blown off
by bombs
maybe they have bought cigarettes or candy bars
I don't know who they are or where they come from
but they walk
in the glare of my headlights
as I wait for the light to turn green so I can drive
on into the factory where I will make parts
for the Air Force planes
that will take boys like them to Iraq
and as the gas pumps
and their metal legs shine
I look over at the 20-storey VA hospital
full of boys like the 2 in my headlights
and I would like to quit my job
but I am 56 years old and not sure where I will get another
just like I'm sure these boys walking past my car
toward the VA hospital were so desperate
for a job they joined
the Army
and they walk off into the darkness
where they will never know who I am
or how deeply they have touched my heart
and the light turns green
and for a moment I refuse
I refuse to go forward until the pile of cars behind me
are honking
like mad and of course I drive on into the morning darkness

the darkness
of convenience stores and gas pumps and job ads
and metal legs
the darkness
where the sun will never
rise.

Concrete Forest Floor

There is a palm tree outside our machine shop tin door
its fronds
point toward the sky as we bend over vices
and scrape stinking steel chips out of the grooves
in our steel machine tables
I have looked at it so long
as my machine chews steel and the time clock ticks
I know each line in its bark
each shade of its red-golden fruit
each squirrel
running up its trunk
and now each day as I drive into work I see tree branches
twisting and dancing and reaching for sky
pine needles
waving in moonlight
towering eucalyptuses
catching the first rays of the rising sun in their leaves
I take them to work
and plant them around my machine beside 10-ton cranes
swinging block and hook and chain
and pounding 30-foot-high
2-ton drop hammers and men
riding wire cage elevators up the faces of 40-foot-high
standing machine beds like steel cliffs
their green leaves
and needles let me breathe deeply
as I cut and measure and polish steel hard and cold
as stone
they were there
long before the first engine turned
their leaves waving in a wind that blew
long before
the pyramids
their breathing leaves their thirsty roots
their sun-drenched tops

and I sweep up their dropped leaves and pine cones
along with the steel chips strewn across the concrete floor
at the end of each day
and dump them in the oil drum chip bins
sad
no one else in this shop can see them
glad
for this forest
in my soul.

Someday There Will Be Machine Shops Full of Roses

The owner of the machine shop calls me into his tiny
windowless office
again
we sit
staring at each other across a dark wooden desk
I want to tell him
I went to college too
had a mother who wanted me to be a doctor or a lawyer
or a company president
like him
but I am a machinist
and we are discussing me putting out more parts per hour
on the 3 machines I run
and he wears a spotless pressed white shirt
and I have black machine grease all over my ragged sweaty
tank top
I want to ask him if he has read Spinoza Aristotle
Confucius Homer Sophocles Shakespeare
Goethe Marx Darwin Tennessee Williams
lately
or written 2 thousand poems
and 7 novels
like I have
I want to tell him that I'm trying to give machinists
and pounding oily machines and taps and cutters
and tin walls and bosses like him their place in literature
and history
but he says I need to put out 10% more parts per hour
and he is looking at a glass display case
full of the shiny brass and steel and beryllium copper parts
we machinists make
mounted on his wall
and I don't think he's read Shakespeare in a long time
if ever

I want to read him my poem
about bringing some roses into the machine shop
and setting them in a glass of water
on my workbench
and ask him if he doesn't think there's a place
for poetry
in the machine shop
but he is tapping a pencil angrily against his desktop
and glaring at me waiting
for me to tell him how I will raise my production rate 10%
and I know I will never be able to read him
any of my poems
it looks like his place in literature and history
will be a lot less interesting
than it might have been.